First a Friend:
the
Life and Legacy
of
Alvan and Ardys Thuma

CAROLYN KIMMEL

First a Friend:
(*Kusaanguna, Wakali Mweenzuma*)

the
Life and Legacy
of
Alvan and Ardys Thuma

*Medical Missionaries to Zimbabwe
and Zambia*

Book Cover Design: Janae Thuma
Printed by CreateSpace, an Amazon company

DEDICATION

This book is dedicated to the grandchildren of Alvan and Ardys Thuma and their descendants. You are part of the wonderful legacy your grandparents left on this earth. May this account of their lives give you the motivation to leave your own legacy.

Note from the Alvan and Ardys Thuma family:

To Carolyn, our sincere thanks for your willingness to visit Zambia and meet the family friends in the Macha community. Thank you for the work of listening and then graciously and thoughtfully writing and re-telling the many stories of Mom and Dad.

There are innumerable stories which could be told involving uncelebrated men and women (around the world) who faithfully follow or followed the call of Christ in their daily lives, not gaining recognition or accolades for their obedience and faithfulness. As Mom and Dad would say "To God be the Glory, great things he hath done".

"As usual,"

Meryl, Phil, Wanda and Barbara

CONTENTS

MAP OF AFRICA

Map Source: http://d-maps.com/m/africa/afrique/afrique16.gif

Foreword by the Author

When Phil Thuma asked me to go to Africa as part of my attempt to write his parents' biography, my first response was "NO." Of course I didn't say that to him immediately, but that's what I thought in my mind. There was no way I was going to get all those shots, subject myself to a days-long trip, deal with another culture and basically, venture so far, *far* outside my personal comfort zone.

To Phil, I simply queried "Couldn't I just Skype those people?"

It's laughable to me now that I would have hesitated one moment in saying "yes!" to his invitation. When I look back at all the blessings that are mine because I stepped out in faith to go where God was calling me to go – just for three weeks – I shudder to think what I would have missed:

The hilarity of traveling with Elaine Thuma, discovering I love baboons after meeting them up close and personal at Victoria Falls, listening to John Spurrier talk about so many things so many evenings, seeing first hand Esther Spurrier's ministry among the African women, witnessing the C-section birth of a precious African baby, meeting so many memorable people, teasing Phil Thuma for just being "Phil," introducing my daughter Olivia to a country where she hopes to one day be a nurse, winning a national writing award for a story I would write about Macha and I could go on . .

The story of how God persuaded me to go to Zambia is pretty amazing; I just have to share it with you.

I met with three of the four Thuma siblings – Phil, Wanda and Barb – a couple of days after Thanksgiving 2012 and we talked about their desire to put down into words the extraordinary lives of their parents. Extraordinary – that's my word, not theirs, but after you read their story, I think you will agree. People had been telling them for years that someone needed to write their parents' story and they were hoping I would agree. They also really wanted me to go to Zambia to see Macha Hospital with my own eyes and interview Zambians who remembered their parents.

I came home from that meeting and told my husband, "I am not going to Zambia."

But as time went on, I began to pray in earnest about it simply because I felt this irritating nudge that I couldn't ignore. In December, I woke up in the middle of the night and said, "OK, Lord, if You want me to go Africa, I can do it. I can! But You are going to have to give me a concrete sign. OK, Lord? I'll be watching for it."

The very next day I was cleaning up around the house and found a TIME magazine on the coffee table. I picked up this issue to flip through it and see if I had read it already. The magazine literally fell open on my lap and in the middle of the page, there was a boldface drop quote that said, **"In the end, we all have to go to Africa."**

I looked up and felt goose bumps standing out on my arms.

"OK, God, here it is in black and white – my concrete sign," I said out loud. I went to my husband and said, "Honey, I guess I'm going to Africa."

I wish I could say that God always communicates with me in such an obvious way!

People often ask me what impressed me most about my trip.

Africa certainly was full of wondrous sights – like an elephant shaking a palm tree so violently between his tusks that it sounded like thunder to bring down his dinner of palm fruit, Victoria Falls spilling over an impossibly wide expanse of cliff, a nighttime sky illuminated with brighter stars than I've ever seen in the smog-filled American sky, a precious baby pulled from a young mother's abdomen after some tense moments of fetal distress.

But, in Africa, I also saw some sobering sights – postage stamp-sized homes with scant furnishings, little children with torn clothing, countless shoes with not much left but the soles, exposed plumbing, torn plaster, skinny dogs, dirty water, flies on hospital patients . . . and yet, smiles, always smiles.

That's the thing that impressed me most . . . people have so little yet they are truly grateful they have anything and that thankfulness spills out of them like a fountain of pure joy! For them, life is a gift, not a given.

It's impossible to spend time at Macha and not be inspired. Life is hard and uncertain there, but it's joyful, so unexpectedly joyful! There's joy in the hard work that pays off; joy in the persistent faith that sees a crisis through to answered prayer; joy in the camaraderie that grows swift and strong in challenging conditions; joy in living out the call that God has put on your life.

I think part of what makes the story of Alvan and Ardys so compelling is that it isn't about a perfect, "holier than Thou" couple who gladly followed a call to Africa and loved every minute of it because God called them there. No, it's about two people just like you and me who obeyed God's call despite their human frailties and accomplished great things, thanks to their perseverance, their faith and God's grace in their lives.

That's something we all have in common with them – we are all imperfect and constrained by our humanness. But with God's help, we can accomplish much. Their lives stand as a testimony to that.

Before you begin reading, there are two things I want to note. First, each chapter begins with an italicized introduction based on truth but bearing some fictional embellishments of dialogue and detail.

Secondly, I would like to thank Esther Spurrier for translating the hymns that appear in Tonga at the start of each chapter. Thank you, Esther and John, for opening your home to me while I visited Zambia and thank you, Thuma family, for your support of this project and for trusting me to tell your parents' story. It's been my privilege.

Carolyn Kimmel

Prelude

August 12, 2009

The dusty, washboard road stretched before them like an endless runway. Jostled up and down as the car strode over the bumps, Phil Thuma and his wife, Elaine, stared straight ahead. Their thoughts were as jumbled as the ride:

The long trip ahead from African bush to American soil.

Dad was gone! How was Mom?

Would the conference they were leaving behind go well without them?

When would they return?

Oh, the long trip ahead!

As Macha Mission Hospital came into view, Elaine squinted to see more clearly. What was going on? Why all the people in the road? Slowly, as the car approached, the people parted to make way even as more people streamed out of the hospital entrance.

A handshake. A hug. Tears. "Mweende kabotu ... Go well," they said over and over again.

Here, the people of the Macha community – hospital staff and village resident side by side – came to honor the man who had come to their land more than 50 years before to make a difference.

Though few of them had actually met Phil's dad, his name was the stuff of legends.

Alvan E. Thuma.

Ohio farm boy. Loving husband and father. Brethren in Christ missionary doctor to Africa. Pioneer in race relations. Former Zambian government medical officer.

But today, the thing that mattered most to the many Zambians who heard the news as it spread like wildfire over the rain-thirsty roads and into the African villages was this: A friend of Macha was lost; some might even say he was a savior of sorts.

With his own hands, Alvan Thuma helped to fire and lay the bricks to give birth to the hospital he designed. With the same hands that expertly and compassionately examined a man, woman or child – for many, the first time a medical doctor

1

ever touched them – Alvan worked alongside his African neighbors to build Macha Mission Hospital.

With it came access to medical care the likes of which these people had never seen. New medicines, medical equipment and procedures improving lives, saving lives.

And more than that, touching lives.

Alvan chatting with a young boy

"Dr. Thuma was my first white friend," recalled Daniel Muchimba as his eyes misted even now – 50 years later – at the memory of the elder Thuma who had supported this freedom fighter and his people in their vision to be independent from British rule.

"Dr. Thuma was so good to the people. He took care of the widows and poor families. Most of the time, he would come and look after my family because my father died," said Selina Moono, who grew up in a village near Macha where Alvan and his wife, Ardys, would go almost every week to see if the family of nine children needed anything.

Even today, Selina remembers the words he left with her so many years ago and recites them with great passion: "Whatever type of problem you face, do not worry because God is in charge!"

Many of those who gave condolences to Phil and Elaine that August day were too young to remember Alvan Thuma.

They stood to honor what – and who – he left behind: A life-saving hospital, a thriving medical community and a legacy in a son whose research and medical approaches have led to a dramatic decline in what was once one of Macha's deadliest enemies, malaria.

Alvan and Ardys Thuma spent only 10 years of their long lives at Macha, yet their reach extended far beyond – to generations of Zambians.

And so here, their story must begin.

‒‒‒‒‒ 🌍 ‒‒‒‒‒

Mbwembede, Mwami, ndeza eno,
Nsijisi kulyaambilila.
Ndiyeeya pele mbondiita.

Mwami Jesu, ndaboola

Just as I am, without one plea,
but that thy blood was shed for me,
and that thou bidst me come to thee,
O Lamb of God, I come, I come.

One
Just As I Am

As the first pink streaks of the morning sky ushered in light to work by, Alvan Thuma gathered his troops, not for war but for construction.
"Andrew,"
"Mpendi (here)"
"Seven?"
"Mpendi"
"Ephraim?"
"Mpendi."
Dr. Thuma called each worker's name on the morning roll to make sure all hands were on deck. Speaking through a village headman, he offered up a morning prayer, "Dear Lord, give us strength for this work and safety for this day. Amen," he said.
"Joe, take the lorry . . . You know what to do. Bring up as many loads of sand as you can this morning," Dr. Thuma instructed the young American who was a leader in the group.
Joe Ginder marveled to himself at the pace the doctor kept. Up at dawn, directing the morning work line of 20 young men, heading a half mile up the dirt road to the existing clinic to see patients until noon, coming back in the early afternoon to organize the next 20 in the afternoon work line and joining in himself with the physical labor. At suppertime, the doctor might head back to the clinic to see more patients before calling it a night.

Joe had to pinch himself a little bit when he took the time to look at his surroundings. For a Manheim, Pennsylvania boy fresh out of high school to find himself working side by side with black men in a remote area of a continent that might as well be the moon, so foreign it was, had to be a dream, didn't it?

But no, it wasn't. Drafted into the Korean War, Joe had asked his uncle Henry Ginder, who was a bishop with the Brethren in Christ Church, to help him secure alternate service in Africa. After a year of moving around between Zimbabwe and Zambia, Joe landed at Macha in 1954. The hospital had just been started, the well only just drilled before he arrived.

"You should've seen it . . . they drilled a hole 900 feet deep and nothing. Doc comes out with a branch and starts witching for water. He found it – hundreds of gallons a minute." If Joe had heard the story once, he'd heard it a thousand times.

Dr. Thuma was a marvel – a medical doctor, a building architect and laborer and a water diviner to boot! He was also the first to use cement, sand and lime in the mortar between the bricks – rather than mud dug from anthills – to discourage termites getting into the walls, Joe knew. Joe had heard the "chatter" among other missionaries – that Doc was "going overboard" by trying this new type of cement.

Even Alvan's own sister, Esther Mann, heard tell was skeptical of what her brother was doing with cement. Her husband, Roy Mann, was using the mud from ant hills to build the hospital at Mtshabezi and trying to do it as cheaply as possible while her brother was doing this modern, expensive thing up north. This was the gossip that made its way to Joe's young ears.

To their credit, however, Roy and Esther were supportive in collecting donkeys for Al to use to pull carts to haul sand and stone. They rounded up local donkeys and sent them on a train to Choma, Joe heard. By then, though, Alvan got a grant to buy a lorry and he didn't need them. In a move that Joe found entirely resourceful, Dr. Thuma sold the donkeys to the government who used them for tsetse fly research.

Large kilns in which to fire the bricks for the new hospital were the first order of business. To make the kilns, Joe and his crew made bricks with clay they dug from ant hills, mixed with water, and put into clay molds. Once the bricks were sun-dried, "We're going to pile them on each other as high as a house!" Joe told his crew. Then the men plastered over the outside of the 50-by-30-foot structures.

For Lazarus Moono Moonga, who was just scraping by as a subsistence farmer in the nearby village of Hamupi, the news circulating in his village and beyond was exciting --- a doctor, a real medical doctor, was coming! And he was going to build a hospital!

Brick kiln for Macha Hospital

When the local brick layer offered Lazarus the chance to work on the brick-making team for the hospital, Lazarus jumped at the chance.

Soon, Lazarus became the supervisor of the process. The crew made 500 bricks in a 14-hour day. Taking mud, clay and adding water, they stamped the mixture down and put it in a mold of three bricks before flipping it out quickly and running back to get more. Sometimes they had 10 to 20 molds going at once. They marked each 100 bricks off with a blade of grass. After several days of air drying, they fired the bricks in the huge kilns. The lorry would bring bricks back to the hospital building site. There, Alvan mixed up his controversial new cement mixture to put between the bricks.

Dr. Thuma would sometimes help ferry the sand himself and he always sat in the back with the workers instead of sitting up front. Lazarus just couldn't get over that. No white missionaries he ever saw acted like that.

7

Because of Dr. Thuma's kindness, Lazarus and many of the other workers only took half of their pay and gave the other half as a contribution to the hospital that they hoped would save many lives in their community.

The Ohio-born farm boy, now husband and father, sailed from New York Harbor to Cape Town in April 1951. There, Alvan and Ardys, with sons Meryl, almost 3, and Phil, 10 months, had to wait two weeks for the arrival of a freighter carrying a Chevrolet Carry All, which was to be the first ambulance for the Brethren in Christ missions in Africa. The family drove from Cape Town to Southern Rhodesia, what is now Zimbabwe – a five-day trip.

The Thuma family in 1951

Alvan Thuma's arrival was momentous enough to earn a mention in the Brethren in Christ's official history, "Quest for Piety and Obedience," by Carlton O. Wittlinger: "The hope for medical doctors moved slowly toward fulfillment. In 1950, three perspective candidates were in medical school, but the most advanced was still a minimum of a year away from readiness for appointment. At that time, Alvan Thuma, M.D., who had recently completed medical school, volunteered to staff the small hospital under construction at Mtshabezi Mission. In the words of a veteran missionary, the arrival of the Thumas on the field a short time later was 'A great day for the African work.'"

In a sermon that Alvan apparently prepared to give before he took his little family off to Africa, he felt compelled to give "a statement of our purpose." His words live on in a small black notebook that contains his sermon notes throughout the years.

"I left the farm in 1940 with the express aim of someday being of service to mankind and helping to spread the gospel . . . I am not interested in a career of tropical medicine, frontier surgery or living in the tropics but rather I'm interested in a cause and that cause is to make Christ known to those who have never had the privilege of accepting Christ," he wrote.

In the denominational periodical, "The Evangelical Visitor" that spring, Alvan confessed he felt a little like Abraham, "setting out, not fully knowing but trusting in God."

For her part, Ardys was feeling the keen sense of a call she knew intuitively was beyond her human ability. "I feel most unworthy and yet greatly privileged to go as the church's and as Christ's ambassador to Africa," she wrote in the "Visitor."

The March 1951 issue of The "Visitor" carried an article about the significant occasion of sending the BIC denomination's first medical doctor overseas. The story included a list of furnishings for the doctor's home for which money was being collected. It totaled $4,488 and included $140 for the kitchen, $420 for three bedrooms and $336 for a 12-cow herd for the doctor.

The Thumas went first to Mtshabezi Hospital in Southern Rhodesia, where Alvan worked for three years. While there, Alvan helped put some additions onto the hospital, such as a kitchen and laundry unit, a three-room African nurses and working girls' home and a two-room house for patients' relatives to stay in at night.

In addition, Alvan reported in the 1951 Mtshabezi Hospital Report in the Handbook of Missions that he had weekly contact with a group of people not reached by other mission efforts. The contact included morning and evening devotions, a weekly service and personal visitation.

"Medical practice lacks some of the finer touches that are found in medical practice in America, but we are not discouraged in the work," Alvan wrote. "'Hitherto has the Lord helped us.' We look to him for daily help and guidance."

Doctor's house at Mtshabezi Mission Hospital - 1951

As time went on, the people in that area came to regard Dr. Thuma as a man who could help them, perhaps, they reasoned, even more than their own traditional doctors.

Ardys learned early on that although she wasn't a constant presence in the hospital itself, her family's mere presence in the village was missions at work. The true grit it took to persevere in Africa was also evident early on. Ardys wrote in September 1952, "Some of our bright spots are not as bright as they should be. In fact they are quite dim and undoubtedly Satan is trying his best to make them go out altogether . . . Oh that we might have many bright spots to brighten up dark Africa!"

Although Alvan did great work at Mtshabezi – completing a women's ward and delivering more than 200 babies a year – it was his next African assignment that would forever link his name with an African Hospital.

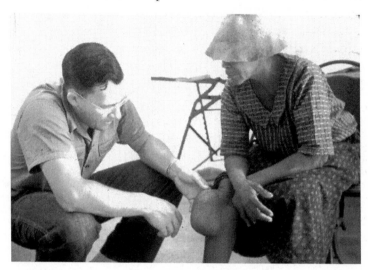

Alvan examining a patient at Mtshabezi Hospital

In a letter home to Ohio, Alvan, reporting on results of the board meeting on May 21, 1954 wrote:

"The minute that most directly affected us is the one that states that after our holiday, Ardys and I will be transferred to Macha Mission in Northern Rhodesia to have charge of the medical work, which means the possible setting up of a whole new unit if finances are available. A few people have congratulated us, but one does not exactly know how to take such congratulations. I guess the safest way would be to interpret it that I now have the status of a qualified builder as well as medical doctor."

The statement reveals a hint of uncertainty, maybe even trepidation, but any such sentiment seems trumped by Alvan's characteristic "take it as it comes" approach to life with a hint of humor mixed in.

Later, son Meryl would remember when his father put elephant bones he had found in front of the hospital, to "advertise that this is a hospital and not everyone comes out alive."

It seems safe to say that Alvan knew he was going to have a huge hand in the building of the hospital where he would then practice. In the 1955 Handbook of Missions, he wrote,

"As of Oct. 1, 1954, the Macha Mission Hospital Unit came into being. Medical work had been carried on for years at Macha under the direction of a nursing sister . . . it was the dream of the mission personnel and the community that a doctor might be placed in charge of the medical work . . . it was evident that the physical plant was too small for the patient load."

Nursing staff with Alvan at old Macha Hospital

Alvan, who would become known for the endlessly fascinating stories he could tell about life in the African bush, didn't have to wait long for his first fodder at Macha. "We seemed to arrive at a very opportune time as the local medicine man had just been poisoned. This man had one time been a school boy at Sikalongo Mission, but it seems the teachings given there by the missionaries had little effect on him," he wrote, immediately relating the story back to something familiar (Sikalongo) for his audience of "Visitor" readers, as expert storytellers know to do.

Alvan went on to describe how the young man had turned to the practice of native medicine and had apparently been very successful at preying on the troubled minds of sick and superstitious natives as he was able to provide for 10 wives and their children.

"I have heard that in numbers there is safety, but this did not pertain to his wives. One of them tried to poison him and he still is not back to his 'work' after five months. With him not 'working,' the patient load at Macha has increased," Alvan wrote.

The new doctor realized that his medicine was, at least initially, viewed in the same manner as the medicine of the traditional healer or witch doctor, but probably even Alvan didn't realize how he was about to change that.

He had already seen a similar change at Mtshabezi. In 1953, Ardys had a written a letter to the "Visitor," telling about the growing confidence they were seeing as people were bringing their sick loved ones to the hospital and not taking them back home, even when they were close to death.

"It shows the people are having more and more confidence in our medicine, for they are willing to leave their people under our care even up to the last," Ardys wrote.

Mission superintendent George Kibler, who was at Macha from 1961 to 1964, recalls villagers came to Thuma for anything and everything. "Someone came to the hospital pulling a car with oxen and asked him to cast out evil spirits because the car had died and 'it won't wake up' – and evil spirits were responsible. They thought for sure Dr. Thuma could help them," said Kibler, now 79.

Often the Thumas would go to the funerals of patients. "This is certainly a great way to sow seed among these people;

and even though we would wish to see immediate results, we can only trust God for the harvest and see to it that we are ever faithful in sowing the seed," Ardys wrote.

Still, it was a struggle to overcome generations of medicine based on spirits and witchcraft. In the same letter, Ardys related the story of a woman who had been sick for a long time before she was finally brought to the hospital. Alvan thought she had tuberculosis and a lung abscess. However, "Her people and she herself believed that she was bewitched. Alvan had me make eggnog for her once a day; he was trying to build her up – and what strength can one get out of this cornmeal porridge only?" We don't find out what finally happened to the woman; Ardys asks for prayer that the family might finally realize that "the power of good is greater than the power of evil."

Alvan conducting a funeral for one of his patients

Several years later, in 1961, Ardys was to receive a strange gift from a medicine man, delivered by a young boy sent to her door at Macha. He came bearing a small bag made from a wild animal pelt that contained roots, herbs and traditional medicines along with a letter that the Thumas still have today. On the envelope, Mrs. Thuma is named as the only one who can open the letter with the instructions "but never disclose anything."

Apparently the local medicine man felt that Ardys should have the traditional powers of a medicine man. The letter gave her instructions on how to do so:

"Patients will know and the 'spirits' will feel your presence and will give your tools the power to work agreeably with you. Your roots and tools must be in the kit at least for a night before put to use or else the spirits will be against your patient. And I tell you, all your patients must see the kit but at all costs must not look into the kit. This is important," the letter commanded.

"From now onwards, never wash yourself with soap. Soap and the contents of this kit do not just go together. Just cleaning cloth may bring misfortune. All the same you are the owner of this doctor's kit."

Whoever sent the kit obviously observed the Thumas often and knew that Phil often had ringworm on his feet. Instead of letting the skin rash go, Phil would pick at it until it bled and got infected. This chronic condition was not lost on the medicine man who wrote, "Even the long troubling sores and wounds on the boys' legs will not resist your power from now."

Did Phil's legs heal up? No. Ardys didn't take the letter seriously, but it does show how much traditional medicine pervaded life at Macha.

Although centuries of folklore and witch doctoring were against them, Alvan was heartened to report that the Northern Rhodesian government was supportive of missions because they didn't have to place a government medical officer there. That meant the hospital could rely strongly on government grants to help with construction of the new structure.

"Things do not happen overnight in Africa; there is work ahead for many days, even years," he wrote. "With the challenge of the task ahead, we pledge ourselves again to the cause of missions in their effort to make Christ known to those who never have heard or accepted Him as their Savior."

Church Executive Board approving Macha Hospital site

The building project at Macha lasted two years. In 1956, when Aaron Chidakwa was home on a school holiday, he was drafted to help Dr. Thuma build the hospital.

"Dr. Thuma was my best friend. He'd say, 'Oh, you have come! Come and help us," said Aaron, now 79, and headman of Chidakwa Village, not far from Macha.

Aaron helped lay the bricks for the men's and women's wards. There was a pool where they dug in the mud to mold the bricks right near the hospital. He also helped build the Thumas' new house across from the hospital.

"Yes, it was a funny shape but no one questioned it," he said with a laugh. "There was a plan drawn up by Dr. Thuma and we followed it. He was the over boss. Whatever he said to do, we did it. No discussion."

Dr. Thuma worked alongside Aaron and the other workers. "He was so kind to us. He had the heart of a sheep. The difference between Dr. Thuma and the others was that he was so kind to people. The other missionaries used to spend time in their houses and they were not approachable. You could go up to Dr. Thuma's door anytime and be answered. It was harder to talk to the other missionaries," Aaron said.

Headman Aaron Chidakwa

Aaron remembers that they would warm themselves by the fire before they began working and Dr. Thuma would come and warm himself too. "He wouldn't tell us to get to work right away," Aaron said.

When Dr. Thuma's sons, Phil and Meryl would come play at the construction site, however, Dr. Thuma was not as kind, Aaron recalled. "He told them, 'Get out of that mud!'"

Keith Ulery clearly treasures his memories of his year spent with Alvan Thuma, helping to build the hospital.

"There was what we'd call an infirmary there and a nurse, Edna Lehman. She fought Doc tooth and nail. She wasn't going to give up her hospital. Doc was always cool as a cucumber about it. He was a very gentle guy; he always had a smile and eventually it came around that he was in charge. Edna left or was transferred," he said with a chuckle.

First A Friend

Keith's ties to the Thumas go back to Ohio, where he knew Alvan's parents. Frank was a big man with a beard; his wife dressed plain. They were Yorkers but they came over to the Brethren in Christ, Keith recalls. Frank had a little car called a Crossley and Keith found it funny as a kid that these plain people drove this spiffy car.

Keith went to Africa on 1-W alternative service in 1955. He was assigned to Macha Mission with Don Zook and Joe Ginder to help build the hospital. He was a freshman at Messiah College at the time and engaged.

"I was with Doc when we staked out the foundation," said Keith, now 77 and living in Dubois, Pa. "He taught me the art of witching for water. He found a stick and used it. He'd walk with it and it would wiggle and jiggle. I must have the 'it' in my body too --- it's something to do with electrodes in your body. Several churches I've pastored, I've helped them find the well."

Alvan's ability to divine water was perhaps honed on the farm in his boyhood days. He makes mention of his ability in a May 1955 letter from Macha to friend Paul Lenhert: "Our first borehole put down on a site chosen by the government geophysicist was drilled to 186 feet and then it yielded only 32 gallons per hour, almost a dry hole. For the next site, I tried a little mulberry twig and walked miles trying to find a good site. They got into water-bearing rock at 130 feet and drilled to 170 feet until they hit blue granite. When they test pumped it, it yielded 960 gallons per hour . . . I'm now thinking of running competition to the government man!" Conveniently, the site, Alvan said, was just 240 yards from the new hospital area.

Next came the chore of getting stone for the foundation. "Doc bought a five-ton truck and we'd go out and gather big rocks that took two to three guys to lift. We dug the foundation, put rocks in and then put mortar on to make a firm foundation," Keith recalled.

Making the mortar was also a process. The cement came on the railroad to Choma, 40 miles away. "Alvan would order it and then the guys would take turns making trips between us to Choma at 40 miles per hour," Keith said. "I'd read a book

18

while I was driving along. We weren't going fast and the only people you met up with were riding a bike or walking."

He remembers how people in Choma would beg for a ride back to Macha and Keith would tell them that if they helped unload the cement, they could come. "Twenty to 30 people would show up at the last minute after the work was all done, wanting a ride and I'd say 'Oh no. You watched us do all this work and didn't help. Come back around next time I have a load to unload.'"

The people were coming to Macha mostly in search of medical care. The work being done at Macha was on the rise, as Alvan noted in his 1956 Handbook of Missions Report: "Six years ago, the operating budget for Macha Mission was $5,922; this past year the combined budget of the mission and hospital exceeded $43,922." Then he added this little editorial comment: "May I add too that I don't think the giving of the Home Church has increased in proportion to the operating budgets of the missions stations."

Alvan described conditions in the previous year – three small wards, 12 by 30 feet with nine beds.

"For the new site, the Government allocated 3,000 British Pounds(about $9,000) for the year, and this was used up in obtaining a water supply, building the doctor's home, making and burning approximately 120,000 bricks for hospital construction and the obtaining of a three-ton Ford Diesel for transport. This transport makes possible more efficient use of the labor crew," he wrote.

Alvan supervised the brick making, using all local labor. Keith described how they had to go out into the bush to get the wood to fire the kiln. One time, a cobra – the size of "a small fire hose" – ran across the road. Keith ran over it twice with the truck, but when he approached it, it rose up and fanned out its neck. The African men with him killed it.

Another time a pride of lions was growling at them; they could hear them. No one wanted to get off the truck to go get wood, but eventually they gathered their courage and took turns to retrieve it. They never did meet up with the lions.

The kiln was big enough to fire 40,000 bricks. They used a tractor and a wagon to gather the wood and bring it in. The kiln had to be fired 24 hours a day and more wood had to be put in every six hours, even during the night. Total firing was a week. When firing was done, they left the mud-covered kiln for 30 days so that the bricks would cool down slowly and not crack.

"It was a very long process. About 50 to 60 of local laborers helped," Keith said.

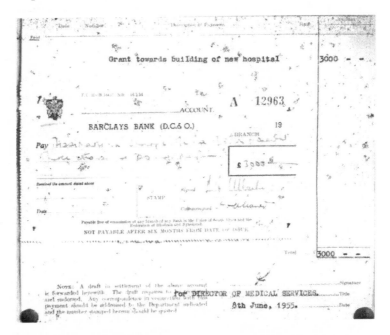

First government check for hospital project

Alvan noted the tediousness and sheer exhaustion of the work in the Handbook of Missions: "Sometimes when the work is only clearing the land of 'bush,' one's vision of the work may become dimmed by physical tiredness. At these times, one needs only to straighten up one's back, take a good look about and into the future to go back to work with new determination. We continue to labor; you pray for us."

Joe Ginder will never forget the stories that Alvan regaled the crew with as they worked. "He had us spellbound, talking about his dating years with Ardys. She lived in Upland and he was in med school in Philadelphia, so he would hitchhike back and forth to see her. He would talk about a truck driver he'd be with for days as he traveled cross country to see her. He was very easy to work with. He was a super man," Joe said.

Alvan returned the same admiration to the young 1-W, writing, "His presence expedited the work and he earned for himself the name Syuumbwa meaning 'lion.' Any oxen named in the community because they have similar spirit to Joe's would be well worth buying and having around."

As hard as Alvan toiled in the hospital and at the construction site, Ardys worked tirelessly at home, much of her time devoted to thoughts of how to feed the growing crowd at her dinner table each day. Not only were nurses and 1-W workers there, it fell to her to host visiting BIC personnel and government officials. She was nothing if not organized, delegating tasks to the household help, planning meals and caring for young Meryl and Phil as well. All the building activity, of course, drew the attention of the local people for miles around.

Sarah Mwaanga, 76, who worked in the Thuma home, remembers when they were building the house and the hospital at the same time. "So many people were happy when the hospital was being built. Before that, we had to go to Choma. People were afraid to go there; people died there."

Martha Muleya, now age 85, recalls when Chief Macha told the villagers that Dr. Thuma was coming and that he would build "a big hut." Everyone was very happy, she said.

Esther Mwaanga, 84, another of the Thuma housekeepers, recalls a big welcome feast for the Thumas. She was very happy because now they have a "big" doctor here, and by this, she means "trained."

In the 1957 Handbook of Missions, Alvan gave a progress report for 1956, noting that he had planned a 273-by-33-foot hospital to house the ever-growing number of patients, but he had not calculated high enough. Where the last six months of

1955 saw 33 inpatients per day, a year later, it was up to 84 inpatients per day and 60 outpatients with no end in sight.

"We now know that the present building program will not take care of those that are now coming to us for treatment, but we continue to build," he wrote.

As the hospital grew, brick by brick, so did Dr. Thuma's reputation among the African people of the surrounding villages.

Andrew Kazemba was a just a boy in 1953 when Dr. Thuma came to town. Andrew lived at Hamoonde, a nearby village and watched in wide-eyed wonder as the hospital was being built.

"Many times" he met Dr. Thuma when he was treated as a boy for stomach problems, head problems and for malaria, which "was not a small disease in those days," he said.

"He was a special doctor. He touched and touched, even if the patient was dirty. He wasn't afraid to touch," said Andrew, now 71, who is very animated and using his hands to demonstrate as he talked. It's remarkable that he is so animated about a man he knew when he was about 11 years old.

"We were just drinking the leaves of the bush with the traditional doctor. It was easy to overdose. With Dr. Thuma, you go on the scale and get the right amount diagnosed for you. Diseases declined under Dr. Thuma. If Dr. Thuma saw you, it was a natural feeling, 'I will get better' – even without treatment," he said.

Comments like these make son Phil Thuma very uncomfortable because, to a scientifically-minded doctor, of course, they are not realistic. But to the African people, who had never had good medical care before, it's easy to see why they attributed god-like status to the missionary doctor who came from a faraway land with these little "magic" pills, the likes of which they had never seen.

Penicillin had recently become available in the U.S. and Alvan brought some of the antibiotic to Africa with him. So here was a trained doctor who examined patients with his hands and gave out mysterious pills that they swallowed and voila, they felt better. It's no wonder they came to regard him as a savior.

Jacob Muchimba, who grew up in the village of Nemfwe and thinks he was born sometime between 1932 and 1936, recalls one time when a group of women walked in from six miles away to see Dr. Thuma, but he was out. So they chose to trek back home rather than be treated by someone else.

He knew people who wanted to receive only the pills that Dr. Thuma gave. They began comparing pills "Yours are brownish. Mine are white. Mine are from Dr. Thuma; yours are not as good," he said.

Though the villagers generally regarded the white missionaries as "unapproachable," Jacob said Dr. Thuma was different. "Missionaries were missionaries; we didn't ask questions . . . they were white people. But Dr. Thuma was a good man; he accommodated people," he said.

Alvan himself noticed the difference in how the hospital was regarded among the villages far out in the bush. He wrote, "The people are becoming more health-minded. They see that a child need not necessarily die because it has the whooping cough or malaria. They see that if a large wound is properly cleansed, sutured and bandaged, the healing time is much shorter. They see those with leprosy and tuberculosis given a new hope in life. They see their complicated maternity cases given a better chance of survival. Incidentally, we make no claims for the spirits that might reside in our medicines, but we thank God that we have modern medicines with which to treat the people."

Perhaps one of the most emotional testimonies to the healing hands of Alvan Thuma comes from Trywell Madubansi, who is the son of the man who was Chief Macha in 1979. Born in 1956, he grew up in village of Mweele and now lives in Dibalizwe.

"I have heard my father tell me this story all my life," he said with great certainty before beginning. "I got sick – I was three months old – I stayed with my father because my parents had quarreled and my mother did not live with us. My stomach was very painful; a twisting pain – "myoonga" – I was in the hospital for three months. I drank ibbwatu liquid with pounded, ground nuts; Dr. Thuma told us to do this and this is how I survived. I got better and went home. Then at 3 years of age, I got the same sickness. That's when Dr. Thuma tried all means to cure my disease, but nothing worked. And he said, 'Let me tell you what to do now.' He told my father to take a root from the Mandazikali tree, put it in water, boil it and drink it. It is more bitter than chloroquine and chloroquine is pretty bitter."

Dr. Thuma realized there was medicinal value in some of the traditional medicines, Trywell insisted. Trywell has taken this root – he has a tree in his village – and boiled it and drunk it most all his life and today, he no longer has the stomach disease that plagued him as a youngster, he said. At the first sign of any stomach pain, however, he takes it.

"I really, really, really feel Dr. Thuma saved my life," he said. "God passed through Dr. Thuma to save my life."

Phil sincerely doubts his show-me-the-medical-studies dad would have recommended a tree root to a patient, but Trywell is insistent. And there's no arguing with the look in his eyes when he talks about Dr. Thuma.

Trywell is moved nearly to tears and a gets a faraway look in his eyes, as if traveling back in his mind to memories of a long-ago time when he hurt and was desperate for help. "I'll never forget Dr. Thuma all my life. Without him, I would not be here."

Whether or not Dr. Thuma really told Trywell's father to boil a tree root and give it to his ailing son is impossible to know since both men are no longer here, but some who knew Alvan think it may have been possible.

"Alvan was always teaching the kids stuff – about bugs, about nature, about how things worked. The thought that he might have experimented with roots doesn't surprise me," said Mim Stern, who was a nurse at Matopo in the mid-1950s when Alvan would come once a month from Mtshabezi to do testing of urine samples for bilharzia, a water-based disease. She would later live in Macha when her husband was mission superintendant.

"Alvan didn't automatically react negatively to alternative therapy, and it may well be that there are roots with medicinal value," said Dr. Sam Brubaker, a medical colleague of Alvan's in post-Africa days. "But he was not at all inclined to buy into fads and much of that alternative stuff he regarded as faddish and not supported by science."

Alvan was, however, known to use a bit of psychology on his patients – we already know he gave out different colored aspirin for different mild ailments for which patients were sure they needed medicine, even though the pills were all exactly the same. So it isn't unreasonable to think that perhaps Alvan exhausted all medical avenues for Trywell's ailment, knew that the villagers placed great stock in the healing powers of a tree root and, knowing it would not hurt the young boy, told his father to use it. The presumed healing powers coupled with Dr Thuma's endorsement might have had the psychological effect of helping heal the boy's stomach pain.

For Alvan, living at Macha meant more than just practicing medicine there; it meant befriending, worshipping with and extending himself to his African neighbors. Trywell remembers that Dr. Thuma had a dairy cow and he supplied each patient with a cup of milk in the morning to increase protein intake.

Often Meryl accompanied his dad out into the bush to make a friendly visit. "When we'd go to a village, they'd call all the men together. The headman would be on a stool, my dad would get a stool and I, as the oldest son, would get a stool. The rest of the men had to sit on their haunches in the dirt. That formed my sense of self at an early age," Meryl said.

Jesse Mwaanga, 81, Headman of Mizinga village (named for his grandfather) sits on a small stool in a dusty, time-worn village where children and adults gather around, openly staring at their visitors, and intensely interested in our conversation – even though it is of things that took place long before they were born.

Jesse said he was very happy to discover there was a doctor coming who was not a woman – a reference to nurse Edna Lehman.

**A Holstein cow, kept for its milk, resting outside Macha
Hospital**

"If Dr. Thuma touched you, you really felt like you were
touched by the hand of healing," he said. "He would go get
medicine and the people were healed."

Jesse is one of many older Zambians who personally attest
that just the touch of Alvan's hand was enough to make him
feel better. True or not, these accounts are worth reporting
because they were so widely believed.

Prior to Dr. Thuma coming, the way people experienced
medicine was through a traditional healer, a man with no
training who never examined the sick but just told them what
was wrong and gave them herbs or tree roots. To be touched
by a trained medical doctor was a huge paradigm shift.

Jesse also recalls taking his sick baby to Dr. Thuma and the
babe being made well.

He saw the hospital being built and attested that he knew
Dr. Thuma very well because of his close proximity to the
hospital --- Mizinga Village is the closest village.

"He was a good man. I can't remember him ever wearing a gloomy face. He liked to talk; he was a social man," he said. "When Dr. Thuma left, I felt everything was going bad; that the hospital was dying," he said.

Author interviewing Jesse Mwaanga near Macha

He knew there were other doctors following, but no one like "the old man."

Ruth Munkombwe, born in 1936 in Maliko Village and treated by Dr. Thuma for malaria, concurs, "He was a very good man. If you were not treated by Dr. Thuma, you felt like you were not treated at all."

The people of Macha and the surrounding villages were surely helped by this stranger from across the ocean who came and lived not only in their village but in their hearts, but at what cost to him? To his wife? To their future?

----- 🌍 -----

Ndalipeda kuli Jesu,
Ndalipeda lyoonse.
Njoomuyanda, njoomusyoma
Njoomuponena Mwami

All to Jesus I surrender;
All to him I freely give;
I will ever love and trust him,
in his presence daily live.

Two
I Surrender All

The sound of a single gunshot pierced the morning sky in Hamumvwanga, a remote village far out in the African bush.

Lameck Chimbongwe glanced at his mother. Their eyes mirrored each other's fear.

"Koya!" she told him. "Go!"

Running as fast as he could, Lameck set out in the direction of the shot, kicking up dust in his wake.

There, up ahead, he saw his father and felt a surge of relief, but it was only momentary . . . Could that be? A leopard? He blinked hard. What was under it? His father's hunting dog. Pinned.

"Don't go after it," Lameck pleaded with his father, but the seasoned kudu hunter would not be outwitted, even by one of nature's most formidable beasts.

As Lameck's father approached, the leopard dropped the dog and, in a flash, had the old man pinned on the ground. In what seemed like an unfathomable move to his young son, his father grabbed the leopard's tongue with his hand so it could not bite his face.

Lameck seized his father's spear and plunged it into the leopard's hide. The hit was enough to stun the leopard into submission long enough for the father and son team to kill the animal with an axe.

Checking to make sure his father was okay, Lameck sprinted back to the village, intent on getting his bicycle to haul his father back home. Adrenaline pumping hard, he spewed out the story to his mother in short, choppy phrases. Word was sent to Macha Hospital to bring a car out to the bush --- a 12- to- 15-mile ride --- so that his father could be taken in for care.

Not long afterwards, Lameck was surprised to see three men approaching on foot; Dr. Alvan Thuma leading the way.

"We couldn't get any farther than the school," Alvan told the worried family. They had walked the last two miles on foot.

Dr. Thuma bent over the crumpled man and began to touch his sore hands tenderly. Perhaps this was the first time that a doctor ever touched him. Before Dr. Thuma arrived, the villagers were used to their traditional doctors, who looked at their patients from an arm's length away and prescribed a set of instructions that often involved boiling up tree roots. These "doctors" had no schooling and learned their medicine from information passed down through the generations.

Dr. Thuma assured the worried family that their patriarch would live . . . and that being the case, he had an idea.

Could they please re-enact the attack because, wow, these would make great pictures!

Alvan was known to restage some of his more exciting exploits in order to have dramatic pictures to show when he was home on furlough, telling about his adventures and raising support to continue his good work with Brethren in Christ World Missions.

The old man was game; he had never had his picture taken before. So they took the dead leopard and draped him over Lameck's father while Alvan shot a series of photographs. Next, the men, Alvan included, carried Lameck's father to their waiting car and began the slow and bumpy ride back to the hospital, where he was admitted for a week. He recovered but lived just four more years until heart disease claimed his life.

Tears cloud Lameck Chimbongwe's eyes as he retells the story of more than a half century ago.

"Dr. Thuma saved people," he said. "He was a humble person who had a lot of kindness toward people."

It's obvious the details of the story are still vivid in this Zambian elder's mind. Now 86 and nearly blind, his entrance to our interview is striking. He is led to our chairs outside his home, clutching the end of a cane that is held by the guiding hand of a young boy. He has glaucoma and sees only white since 2002, he said. Lameck appears to have dressed up for the occasion. He wears a black suit jacket, a blue shirt with a cream-colored scarf at his neck and a fetching leather hat.

Lameck Chimbongwe talking about Alvan Thuma

This story, as much as any still told around fires and between stools out in the Zambian bush, illustrates the many facets of Dr. Alvan Thuma – and why he is so beloved by the Macha community even now, more than 50 years after his departure.

This story shows Alvan's commitment to his work – that he would drop whatever he was doing at the hospital that morning to drive out to the bush instead of waiting for the injured to be brought to him. Lameck was surprised that the area's only doctor had himself come to the scene.

It shows Alvan's natural curiosity – that upon hearing of an incident involving a leopard, he wanted to be first on the scene to see it firsthand.

It shows Alvan's humility – that he, a learned doctor and important community resource, would walk into the bush when the car could no longer go.

It shows his compassion – that he took time to comfort Lameck and his family, to assure them that their beloved father and husband would not die. It was this kind of intimate interaction that would build a trust among the Zambian people that continues to this day.

It shows his medical prowess and resourcefulness – that he could examine and attend to a medical emergency in a remote area, far removed from hospital equipment and supplies.

And it also shows Alvan's sense of humor and perhaps awe at the circumstances in which he found himself – that he would, after finding the wounds not life-threatening, re-stage the event so that he could take pictures! What a gripping presentation this would make on his next furlough!

Later, Alvan would buy the leopard skin from Lameck's father. The retelling of this story today – for, no doubt, the hundredth or more time – solves a mystery in the present Thuma household. A leopard skin at Phil Thuma's house had no story linked to it until now.

"I think we have that leopard skin!" exclaimed Elaine Thuma, Phil's wife, after hearing the story this sunny, July morning in 2013, 55 years later.

Perhaps Alvan bought the skin so that, for the rest of his life, he would have a visual reminder of what was surely one of the most interesting experiences of his life in the African bush.

Although other missionaries had been sent to Africa before him, Alvan Thuma stands out not only because he was the first doctor, but also because he showed great human compassion and a genuine interest in assimilating into the lives of the African people, learning from them as much as they were learning from him.

Years later, Zambian BIC Bishop Thuma Hamukang'andu visited Alvan at Messiah Village in Mechanicsburg, Pa., where he lived the last decade of his life and asked, "Why do you think you had such an impact?"

Alvan replied, "I chose to stand between the blacks and the whites, even though people didn't understand it. Even my fellow missionaries misunderstood that . . . but if I wanted to be valuable, I had to do it. I traveled all the way from America to Africa and then why would I want to run away from the people I came to help?"

The Bishop's own story bears witness to the doctor's intentions.

"He saved my life," said the 58-year-old Zambian who grew up close to Macha in Sikufweba. "My father told me when I was a child, after a week, I became sick. My parents tried all ways of treating me and they were losing hope."

His parents had taken him to the traditional doctor in their village, but still their newborn son struggled for life. At three months, they took him to Macha Hospital, where Dr. Thuma treated him successfully.

"My father was so excited I recovered that he requested if he can name me after him and he said yes," Bishop Thuma said. "My father was a teacher. He always told me that 'Dr. Thuma was closer to God than any other person I've ever met. He is such a good doctor that God must be very close to him.'"

The legacy of his name is not lost on the BIC church leader. "Tuma" is a word in the tribal language of Tonga that means "to send." When Bishop Thuma graduated from Sikalongo Bible Institute in 1978, it seemed more than fitting that BIC Bishop Frank Kipe commissioned him, saying, "Thuma, ndaku tuma," which meant "Thuma, I am sending you."

For those whom Dr. Alvan Thuma was sent to help – generations of Zambians who still name their children after him – his humility and compassion are unforgettable. Perhaps it is because he was so often there in those precious moments when the pendulum swings uncertainly between life and death.

Decades later, Lameck Chimbongwe still remembers the day in 1975 when Dr. Thuma again touched his life.

Alvan returned to Macha Hospital that year for 12 months of volunteer service. Lameck's wife had fallen ill with diarrhea and anemia. Lameck drove her to the hospital and he recalls that Dr. Thuma came outside on the veranda to meet the car and instructed him to take her inside. She had with her their 8-month-old baby girl, who was nursing.

"Dr. Thuma told the nurses that the child should not nurse on her anymore because she was too weak. So Dr. Thuma went and brought a bottle of milk for the child," he said.

His wife died that evening.

Again, tears come at the memory.

Knowing that the care of the baby was beyond Lameck's ability, the hospital chaplain told Dr. Thuma that someone was needed to care for her. Dr. Thuma explained the need to two German and Dutch nurses who were on staff and they found a girl from Lupata village to help care for the baby in the immediate future. Then, the nurses themselves took the tiny girl and raised her until their terms of service at the hospital were over years later. They returned the girl to Lameck when they left and he thankfully welcomed his daughter home, healthy and well cared for.

"That's why I always remember Dr. Thuma. I am very thankful for him," Lameck said.

Today, fittingly, Lameck's son, Misheck, works for staff members of Macha Research Trust, founded by Alvan's son, Phil Thuma. Misheck, gardener extraordinaire, shares his father's warm personality.

"I've heard the leopard story dozens of times growing up," Misheck said with a grin that overtakes his face. "It's a good one."

Keith Ulery, who was a 1-W assigned to Macha for alternate service from the war from 1955 to 1957, recalls another Alvan adventure story, albeit somewhat grisly.

"A boy was killed, beaten by his father, and the government called on Doc to do an autopsy on him. Alvan asked me if I wanted to see an autopsy and since I was always interested in medicine, I said, 'Sure,'" Keith said.

The pair traveled to Choma, where Alvan would do the autopsy at the government hospital located there. Knowing Keith's interest in medicine, Alvan decided to give a little anatomy lesson while he worked.

"Doc opened the head; he sawed off the top and pulled back the skin and lifted back the top of the skull to show me the brain. He showed me where all the different nerves were and what they did. Suddenly there was a knock on the door and it was the police, saying someone was there to identify the boy. Doc said, 'Good grief, now what will we do?' He quick put the skull back on and pulled the skin back over his skull so he had a face. He had me to hold a towel at the top of the boy's head. We covered most of the body up and let the father come in," Keith recounted. "It was an interesting experience. Of course it was a warm day and there was no air conditioning and the smells weren't the greatest . . . With Doc, you never knew what was coming next!"

Yet Keith turns reflective and even eloquent when summing up who Alvan was: "When a patient was in front of Alvan, that person felt like he really cared. That was a gift that Al had. He was a most humble man for all the gifts and talents he had. There are rewards for following God. There are sacrifices to be made. There are heartaches, but God rewards you for putting Him first in life."

Alvan Thuma had good role models of what it meant to put Christ at the head of one's life. Born into a conservative Brethren in Christ family on December 19, 1921, Alvan was the tenth of 11 children. The large, happy clan that Frank and Fanny Thuma shepherded grew up on a farm in Miami County, Ohio. Known in the family as "the Route 55 farm," it was located not far from Troy, Ohio, and consisted of about 120 acres. The family worshipped at the Pleasant Hill Brethren in Christ Church.

Perhaps Alvan got his work ethic and innovative spirit from his dad. It's said that Frank Thuma, upon buying the farm from his father, built a larger barn, silo and milk house, added at least one room to the house and installed one of the first indoor bathrooms in that area of the county. There, Frank and Fanny's 11 children were born between 1902 and 1923 in this order: Ruth, Elizabeth, Leah, Benjamin, Mary, Esther, David, Daniel, Fannie Naomi, Alvan and Anna.

As recounted by Alvan's nephew Robert Mann, Frank had trouble paying the bills during the Depression and went bankrupt, due to an outbreak of cholera. The large family moved around to several farms in the area as Frank worked as a hired man or rented from the owners. Later, in 1935, daughters Elizabeth and Mary pooled their wages from their jobs and together bought a farm north of Pleasant Hill. This, the "Route 48" farm became the new home of the Thuma family and Frank and Fanny lived there the rest of their lives. Alvan was 14 when the family moved to the Route 48 farm.

**Thuma family reunion 1958 (Alvan and sibs in middle
row with parents Frank and Fannie)**

Interestingly, it was after Frank Thuma lost his first farm in the Depression that he seemed to gain a deeper spiritual life – and this would have been the side of his dad that Alvan likely most remembered. Gone were the days where Frank thought it was important that all his livestock be registered and that his farm buildings be large and impressive. Now, he was zealous for the Lord.

Although Frank's education ended at grade 8 and Fanny's at fifth grade, they passed on a love of learning and knowledge to their children. Esther Mann, in her biography, says that her dad subscribed to the National Geographic . . . Could this have been the means by which young Alvan first set his eyes on the African plain that would one day become his home?

The Thumas were the first of the Pleasant Hill BIC families to not only allow but encourage their children to go to high school, even college. Alvan would go on to medical school and four of his sisters trained in nursing.

The Pleasant Hill congregation placed great emphasis on missions and often welcomed furloughing missionaries to speak. Surely Alvan sat in the pews on many occasions and heard about the impact that a calling overseas could have on one's life and faith.

Could he have ever imagined that he would be the first BIC missionary doctor to follow a call overseas?

At age 14, Alvan accompanied his parents and siblings to a train station in Piqua, Ohio on a cold January night in 1936 to say good-bye to sister Esther, who was headed to Africa to serve as a nurse. Later, Alvan would say this experience helped influence his own decision to become a missionary doctor.

"A call to service is in the Thuma gene and you're often called to do it internationally. Some people are designed by God to do that kind of work and when you do, you feel fulfilled," said Ron Herr, son of Alvan's sister, Mary.

Ron recalls growing up in the same Pleasant Hill congregation and, years later, being in the pew to hear Alvan and Ardys Thuma, home on furlough from Africa, speaking about their work.

"Aunt Elizabeth was very proud of what her siblings achieved. She was thankful and pleased that Alvan and Ardys were missionaries and I, in turn, had a very positive attitude toward them," Ron said. (His feelings toward cousins Phil and Meryl were not quite as warm, especially when they were home on furlough and eager to try out all his "toys." Ron especially worried about the way they rode his new 1956 three-speed Schwinn bicycle with reckless abandon!)

Ron, who grew up near Grandma and Grandpa Thuma and worked closely with his grandpa on the farm, doesn't remember them talking much about the exploits of their missionary doctor son.

"If Grandpa were to say, 'Mission accomplished,' they would be looking for those things in the context of whether their children were walking with the Lord," Ron later said. "I believe they were very happy when they saw Uncle Alvan went to college, pushed forward and became accepted to medical school and when the BIC Church Mission Board accepted him as the first Brethren in Christ doctor to go overseas, I think they must've been very happy. I don't think I ever heard them brag about it, but I think they were thankful in their hearts . . . They saw God's goodness working through their son serving others . . . and in the ditches digging in the dirt also."

Interest in medicine began early for Alvan Thuma. As a child, his job was to help the veterinarian when he came to the farm to inoculate and examine the animals. Alvan enjoyed this assignment and later, in high school, his biology teacher encouraged him, saying, "You're smart enough. You should become a doctor for people."

After high school graduation, Alvan wasn't quite sure whether he should head to college or get a job. His sister, Elizabeth, worked for Hobart, a food mixer company in Troy, Ohio. Because Alvan was interested in going overseas, he interviewed to be a typist/clerk for Hobart in South America. He planned to take the typing test and if he passed, he would get the job.

Coincidentally – although he would come to view it as no coincidence at all – he was trimming trees near the Fairview BIC Church cemetery before his scheduled typing test when a tree fell and smashed his finger. He went at the appointed test time and explained that his finger was smashed and asked if he could he take the test another day. The answer was no – and he missed that job opening.

"So he decided to go to college and he often talked about God allowing things to happen in your life that would change the course of your life," Phil said.

When it came time to select a college, Alvan didn't want to travel the same path as his older brothers, Ben and Dan, who studied at Messiah College. He chose Upland College in California.

There, during fall revival meetings, he fully gave himself to the Lord for whatever work He would have for him to do. The next fall, Alvan was baptized at the Upland BIC Church and formally joined the BIC denomination.

Being a conscientious objector during World War II, Alvan transferred to Goshen College, hoping he would be deferred so he could continue his education as a pre-med student.

He did indeed graduate and applied to Hahneman Medical College in Philadelphia, where he was accepted to begin in January 1944. He began teaching math and science at Newton High School in Pleasant Hill, Ohio, for the six months in between, but just a month before his scheduled departure for medical school, the draft board ordered him to go to Cincinnati for induction, despite his pre-med deferment.

"He realized he was destined for camp as a conscientious objector for perhaps as long as four or five years, since no one knew when the war would end. A medical education now seemed to him out of the question since he was already in his early twenties," wrote his wife, Ardys, in the BIC history book, "My Story, My Song."

Calling it "one of God's greatest miracles of the 20th Century," Ardys, who met Alvan at Upland College where she was also a student, described how Alvan went for a physical by several military doctors, answered questions about why he was a conscientious objector and what he wanted to do with his medical education and then, for no apparent reason, Alvan was given a 4F classification, which meant he was physically unfit to serve.

There was nothing wrong with the strapping young man, but God's hand on his life was already apparent. God had plans for Alvan Thuma in Africa and no one – not even the U.S. government – was going to stop those plans.

Ironically, it seemed like the Brethren in Christ might stop him if it could.

There was a streak of stubbornness that served Alvan well in carrying out the calling on his life. Although he was humble and gentle and kind, he was also principled and when he felt a conviction about something, he clung to it like a junkyard dog on a meaty bone.

Early evidence of this was seen when Alvan decided to be baptized while a student at Upland. Like many educated students, he had begun sporting a necktie and did not shed it when he returned home to Pleasant Hill, asking to be baptized in his home church.

His bishop informed Alvan that he would have to remove his tie if he wanted to be baptized; a tie was not in keeping with the traditional plain clothing of the BIC in those days.

Using perfectly logical sense, Alvan declared that it would be hypocritical to remove his tie just for baptism or Sunday services because he was a medical student and would have to wear a tie to class. He was refused baptism in Ohio so he came back to California, where the BIC churches were more progressive, and the bishop there baptized him with a tie, no problem.

Then, years later, when Alvan and his wife, Ardys, presented themselves for missionary service before the BIC board, they were asked why Ardys didn't wear a head covering. She had abandoned it, except on Sundays, because she was a public school teacher.

"Well, they couldn't have a missionary who didn't believe in wearing a head covering. But my husband told them that as a teacher, I couldn't wear it, and, Lord knows, if I felt the need to pray anywhere, it was at school during the day, and I felt my prayers got through even though I didn't have a covering on!" Ardys said during an interview in 2005. Because Alvan was on record as wearing a tie and – gasp – attending movies and operas in Philadelphia, where he was a medical student, he had "black marks" on his membership record in Ohio, his wife said. Therefore, the conference would not recommend him for missionary service. Subsequently, Alvan asked Bishop Jacob Bowers, who presided over the Souderton, Pa. church, if he would recommend him for missionary service if they were to transfer their membership to the Souderton church. "Of course," Bowers said, and so they did. "It's laughable now," Ardys said. "But it was upsetting then."

It was the red tie that Alvan wore to a subsequent BIC General Conference – and his conviction that there was nothing ungodly about it – that cost him the chance to have his medical schooling paid for by the denomination in exchange for promising a certain number of years as a missionary doctor.

"This guy's got a streak in him if he wears a red tie to appear before the mission board that he knows doesn't believe in ties!" said Dr. John Spurrier years later when reflecting on the man who built the hospital where Spurrier would spend more than three decades as a missionary doctor.

Also, at the time he applied to the mission board, Alvan had a life insurance policy, a practice that the BIC didn't believe was appropriate. As son Phil remembers his father telling him, Alvan asked Paul Lenhert, a BIC doctor, to hold his life insurance policy and pay the premium for him while he was on the mission field so that when Alvan was asked, "Are you paying for life insurance?" he could say no.

Alvan's youngest daughter, Barb Thuma, sums up that side of her dad as a "rebel rouser." Phil described it as "one who was willing to push the boundaries."

"He was sort of stubborn. Once he felt he was doing something right, he did it," Barb said.

That conviction that he was right could have, in other men, spawned arrogance, said Alvan's older daughter, Wanda Thuma-McDermond.

"There's a quiet arrogance in the Thuma family; a 'we're all pretty intelligent and we know it' type attitude. I think if my father had not been a Christian, with the possibilities of his position as a physician, he perhaps could have been very arrogant," she said.

"Maybe he was smug, not arrogant," Mim Stern, now 86, whose husband was superintendent of Macha Mission for a time, assessed. "He was confident. He was brought up with hard work and brains – it was a very good combination . . . He loved reasoning – figuring out how something works and why, and I think he implanted that in his boys. I can still see them bent over bugs and one of them saying, 'Now this one doesn't go as fast as that one. Why do you think that is?'"

Glenn Schwartz, a 1-W sent to help Alvan in 1962, remembers hearing that Alvan was a little concerned about a female doctor coming to Africa.

"Alvan had been the only medical doctor for years and then this woman doctor – Virginia Kauffman – came along. He thought, "Now how am I going to distinguish myself?' So he grew a beard! It was something he knew she couldn't do!" he said with a laugh.

Alvan loved a good story and he was a grand storyteller.

"He was full of stories and he was a very dramatic storyteller," said John Spurrier, who spent a year learning the ropes from Alvan in 1975 when John arrived in Macha and Alvan was there for a year of voluntary service. "He would tell one story about how he was riding a bike and a black mamba snake, which is very big and deadly, was going along the road. As he told the story, the hairs would stand up on my arm; he was such a great storyteller!"

The downside? Alvan liked to tell the same stories over and over again. "That story was impressive the first time, but not necessarily the eighth time!" John said with a wide grin.

George Kibler, who was Macha Mission superintendent from 1961 to 1964, recalls the story of what happened to his 3-year-old daughter Greta in the Thuma kitchen one night during weekly missionary meeting.

"She came running, saying 'My eye is a snake!' We found there was a cobra in the kitchen and it had spit in Greta's eye!" he said. "Alvan went over to the hospital to get some medicine to put in her eye. They washed her eye out with milk."

This made for a dramatic tale whenever Alvan needed a quintessential "wilds of Africa" story.

Not only did he love to tell stories of his past experiences, but he also added plenty of details, Phil recalled. "A typical story would start something like this: 'It was 5:15 p.m. on the evening of March 21, 1941, the temperature was 48 degrees with a slight drizzle, and I was standing on the outskirts of Abilene, Kansas, trying to hitchhike my way to California with only $1.42 in my pocket.' We used to ask him how he remembered such minute details – and he would just give that smile we all knew – as if to say 'Are you doubting my memory?' For many of his grandchildren, their recollection of him is related to these many stories that he told – mostly from events in his own life – yet never told in a way to impress or give credit to himself."

That truth rang true with many people who knew Alvan later in his life, long after Africa days were past. Doctors with whom he practiced years later in Ohio didn't ever realize he was a highly-decorated medical officer from Zambia or that he had designed and helped build a hospital with his own hands.

"He was so deferential. People never knew he went to formal dinners in Zambia with presidents and prime ministers," said Dr. Sam Brubaker, who practiced with Alvan in Ohio in the 1980s. "He didn't talk a lot about his time in Africa. He didn't make a point to say that he was an expert in Third World healthcare. People would say, 'What experiences Al had! I never knew.' Al was a man much greater than hardly anybody knew. He was so steady, so dependable, a man of his word. The things he said were worth listening to."

Alvan was not one to show his emotions outwardly, his children said.

"My personality is probably more like my dad's ... more stoical, not too emotional, a 'shut up and keep going' attitude," Wanda said.

"He was very stoic," Meryl agreed. "He accepted things as they came."

"Our father was also a practical, matter of fact, 'what you see is what you get' person – he seemed to have had no deep and complex personality traits," Phil said.

Alvan also taught his children not to make much of being sick, they said. If it wasn't going to be fatal, his advice was to just suck it up and move on.

The compassion that so easily flowed for his African patients, however, ran dry when it came to showing much affection to his family. On second thought, perhaps that should be stated the other way around – In contrast to his usual staid nature, Alvan exuded compassion for his African patients; evidence of God's sufficient grace?

"He was a man of his generation. He didn't go around saying "I love you," but I know he did love my mother and us children," Barb said.

Although he undoubtedly faced many a hardship and setback while working in the primitive African bush, Alvan didn't show his anger much either.

"He would never admit he was angry; he would only say he was "half griped." Not sure I ever heard him yell," Barb said.

"He was never one to hold a grudge," Phil agreed.

To those outside the family, like Keith Ulery, it appeared Alvan had "a shell" around him. "You got so close once in a while and he would share some gut feelings, but mostly he was steady as it goes. Nothing really put him over the edge," Keith Ulery said. "He was well suited to be a pioneer missionary doctor with little tools to work with."

"He could handle a saw, a hammer, a plow as easy as a scalpel," George Kibler said. "He was not a proud doctor who was just doctoring. He was helpful to people in every way."

Together, Alvan and Ardys Thuma ministered to families in Macha and surrounding communities.

Lazarus Moono Moonga remembers that Dr. and Mrs. Thuma routinely visited his house because his father was a deacon in the BIC Church. They would help the family, giving them gifts like food and money to supplement their meager resources.

He was really sad when Dr. Thuma left. "I still think of him because of the good things he did," he said. To him and his siblings, Dr. Thuma was like a parent.

When Lazarus became a father himself, he had five sons and then a daughter, similar to Dr. Thuma having two sons and then a daughter. For that reason, Lazarus says he named his "Mutinta" – a term that refers to the first child of a new gender born into a family – "Wanda," just as the good doctor had.

Alvan Thuma lived his faith rather than preached it. Most who knew him said they didn't see him reading his Bible a lot or trying to convert people to Christianity.

When Alvan did preach – as missionaries were expected to do from time to time – his sermons were short, direct and lacked any pulpit-pounding. Alvan's preaching style was in keeping with his lifestyle – actions speak louder than words.

"I remember sometimes people would criticize him for missing prayer meeting – imagine a missionary missing prayer meeting!" recalled Meryl. "And he would say, 'Well, my work is sometimes a prayer.'"

The truth of that sentiment is apparent in a report that Alvan wrote from Mtshabezi in 1953 about a young patient – a 25-year-old mother of two with a third child on the way, presenting at just 95 pounds and complaining of fatigue, weight loss and coughing. The diagnosis: Advanced tuberculosis. Her physical condition was hopeless, Alvan noted, but even more troubling, her spiritual condition was equally void. He began talking with her about the Lord and prayed with her. Three months later, he was called to her hut to talk with her, as she was nearing death.

"Kneeling there in the hut with the lights of the motor car shining in the doorway, I spoke from John 3:15-17 and gave, I believe, one of the greatest messages I will ever preach. At the close, Naka Ina said she was happy, no longer distressed in her soul, and ready to die. As I knelt there in the hut, I thought only momentarily about the teeming tubercle bacilli in the dust and the air. I trusted in Divine protection. Several days later she died . . . no one preached her funeral, I had done that two days earlier."

In a passage of Scripture no doubt familiar to any missionary, Jesus tells his disciples in Matthew 16:25, "If anyone would come after me, let him deny himself and take up his cross and follow me. For whoever would save his life will lose it, but whoever loses his life for my sake will find it. For what will it profit a man if he gains the whole world and forfeits his soul? Or what shall a man give in return for his soul?"

Perhaps Alvan and Ardys Thuma would not have quoted this verse as their life verse or even a favorite, but it could be said that their lives are the essence of Matthew 16 come to life.

People often do amazing things worthy of admiration and respect but to do amazing things in the face of difficult circumstances and to the detriment of one's own comfort and, at times, family relationships . . . is truly amazing; one might even say divinely ordained.

The story of Alvan and Ardys Thuma is the story of two people who sacrificed everything to follow the Lord – physical comfort, affluent lifestyle and to some extent, even the quality of their marriage and their relationships with their children – because they felt His call.

Ardys would write years later in "My Story, My Song," that "A great deal of Al's and my life have gone into Macha Mission Hospital, and parts of our hearts shall always remain there with those people and that work. It was not all easy, however. There were many times of discouragement, but God always gave grace and strength. Even as I write now, tears come to my eyes as I think of those hard, but also very precious, years. Neither of us would ever give them up if we could. They stand as the upmost in our dedication to God."

The Thuma story is also the story of how God not only calls but equips those he calls for the tasks ahead. The Thumas were far from perfect, like all of us, but they accepted the grace and strength offered to them by God to do His work. And in His power made perfect in their weakness, the Thumas found they indeed could call those years "precious."

----- 🜚 -----

Wakatazigwa mumoyo sena?
Mwaambile Jesu, mwaambile Jesu.
Wakatazigwa mumoyo sena?
Mwaambile Jesu alike.

Are you weary, are you heavy hearted?
Tell it to Jesus, tell it to Jesus.
Are you grieving over joys departed?
Tell it to Jesus alone.

Three
Are You Weary?

Ardys Engle put on her prettiest dress and stared at herself in the mirror. Face a little pale, she assessed, and where did that piece of stray hair come from? But her dress was the latest fashion and so, overall, not too bad, she told herself.

She was happy to have the evening off from preparing supper for Doc Weber and his wife. Oh, it wasn't that she didn't love and appreciate their willingness to give her room and board in exchange for her cooking, housework and answering the busy town doctor's phone, but a college girl reveled in a night on the town. So what if it was with her Uncle Paul? Having dinner with her mother's older brother was as close to her real family as she could get at the moment. Her thoughts flew to India before she mentally yanked them back to California. Yes, her parents and sisters were there and she was here. Yes, the hurt at being left behind was still raw. But what good did it do her to dwell on it? She mustered the same resolve she had drawn upon as a 6-year-old girl being sent to boarding school in Darjeeling. Stiff upper lip. Serve others. God first. Others next. Yourself last.

Later that evening, she sat across from Uncle Paul Eyer at a small table in the corner of a favorite restaurant and reminisced about the wonderful trip she took with her grandpa, Isaac Eyer, the previous year. He took her on a tram to Long Beach to see the ocean and visit the Pike, an amusement park. She laughed as she thought of his snow white hair blowing in the breeze on the boardwalk and how it lifted up and down

49

with each note he played so exuberantly on his little pump organ that she hoped one day would be hers.

Uncle Paul laughed with her and then grew serious, as he asked her how she was adjusting to being left behind when her family returned to their mission work in India. Did she like Beulah College? How were her grades? Was it hard to commute and balance school work with working for Doc Weber?

It was fine, Ardys told her uncle. She was doing her part. She understood that her parents couldn't take her back with them – although why they had waited until two weeks before their return to tell her was beyond her comprehension.

"Ardys, always do what the Lord asks of you," Uncle Paul said, locking his eyes onto hers. "I felt the Lord called me to be a minister, but I married a Catholic girl, and I never did become the minister I felt I was called to be."

Suddenly, Uncle Paul broke down and wept. Right there in the restaurant.

The memory of that moment – of watching in disbelief as a grown man dropped his sandwich and wept strong tears of remorse – would never be forgotten by Ardys. And she determined right then that she would never cry those same bitter tears of regret. God first. Others next. Yourself last.

Ardys Engle was born on January 29, 1924 in Upland, California. Ironically, the doctor who delivered her would one day employ her at his home – Dr. Arthur Weber. The roots of her family on both sides went down deep in Brethren in Christ soil. On her father's side, she went back seven or eight generations to Jacob Engle, the founding father of the BIC Church. Her grandparents were among the first young band of BIC families to pull up stakes in Pennsylvania and move to Kansas to plant the first BIC church there. Jesse Engle, one of the first BIC missionaries to set foot on African soil and establish missions work there, was her great-great uncle.

Perhaps the drive toward mission work in foreign lands was passed down in her family along with the rich BIC history.

From her earliest memory, Ardys was a young child growing up in India, where her parents, Charles and Kathryn Eyer Engle were serving as missionaries. Kathryn was in charge of the widow's home and Charles did medical work at the dispensary. Soon, Kathryn was put in charge of Gloven, a rest home in Darjeeling, and spent six months a year managing the home. Ardys was enrolled in Mount Hermon boarding school, in Darjeeling, until 1934, when Gloven was demolished in an earthquake that did severe damage in North India.

From 1932 to 1934, the Engle family lived in Supaul, another of the mission stations. During those years, Ardys gained two sisters, Marylou in 1930, and Phyllis, in 1932. Ardys' separation from the family had already begun; she would come home from boarding school only for the four-month yearly vacation from Nov. 1 to March 1.

Ardys would remember the times of coming home with great fondness in later years. At her father's 100th birthday, she wrote: "You would come on a Friday afternoon after school or a Saturday morning to take me "home" to Gloven for the weekend. We had this monumental mountain to climb from the school to get to what was called the town road . . . As I remember, to go up the mountain was a mile. Then it was another mile though the town to Gloven . . The climb up the mountain was the worst. It seemed straight up and you were an excellent walker and hiker, with legs and feet at least twice my size. So as I tried to keep up with you, sometimes I had to almost run to keep up. Then my head would pound and I'd be out of breath, and I'd want to stop and rest awhile. But you soon wanted to press on. Finally, even in my young years, I found a way to divert your attention so we could pause a little. "Oh Daddy, see the buttercup," or "Daddy, that looks like an insect or butterfly I don't have in my collection. Let's stop and look at it or catch it if we can" or "See that new kind of moss?" or "That looks like a fern I don't have in my collection." You were a true nature buff and this was always a means of getting you to stop when my little legs were tired. I also was very interested in nature around me. I still am. I certainly learned that from you and I thank you for it."

Ardys went on to write that she dreaded the Sunday afternoon trek back to school because she didn't want to leave home. "Many tears were shed the first half hour or so back at

Ardys (R) with her sisters Marylou (L) and Phyllis

school," she wrote. This would be a foreshadowing of the many tears Ardys would cry eight years later when she would be left on another continent altogether.

There came a day when young Ardys felt lonely even in her own home, after her sisters – whom she adored – came along and took up so much of her mother's time. She wrote, "But you were there Daddy to give me that time, love and affection which I sorely wanted and needed."

At school, Ardys, who was striking with her long black curls and very black eyes, was popular and kept many of those friends all her life, according to her sister, Marylou. One was a Norwegian girl named Berit Gausdal (now Oygarden), whom Ardys visited in 1965 in Oslo, Norway. From 1935 to 1936, the Engle family again lived in Saharsa. Both bungalows in Saharsa and Supaul had been indigo planters' homes. They were large and spacious, Marylou recalled.

There too, Ardys longed for human companionship. "In Saharsa, there was a Girls Orphanage, but Ardys was not allowed to play with the girls, which was heartbreaking for her," Marylou recalled.

It was there at the Saharsa Mission during a revival meeting that 6-year-old Ardys knelt in prayer and gave her heart to God.

A tidbit in the 1932 BIC Mission Handbook reveals something about Ardys at age 8: "During the year the general health of the missionary staff has been good for which we thank our heavenly father. Only for the fact that Ardys, the elder daughter of Bro. and Sr. Engle, sustained a broken arm while in school and was in quarantine for chicken-pox, there was very little other sickness."

In 1937, when Ardys was 13, the family returned to the United States on furlough, via Singapore, Marseilles and London, on a Cunard liner. Ardys had a boy friend on this trip who followed her around, much to the consternation of their mother, Marylou recalled. In London, they visited Madame Tussauds wax museum, heard the Salvation Army band at Salvation Hall, and saw the reviewing stands of the recent coronation of King George the VI. Perhaps Ardys formed her love of culture and history on this early trip.

The Engles lived in the missionary home in Grantham, Pa. until after the BIC General Conference, when they drove to California, stopping at many places along the way to give missionary talks. The girls often had to perform, dressing in saris and singing Indian hymns and saying the Lord's Prayer in Hindi.

The next two years were spent in Upland, Calif. in a little yellow house, across from the Upland Brethren in Christ Church on Third Ave. Here, Ardys learned to know her beloved Grandpa Isaac Eyer. Ardys was the only member of the family who played his little pump organ, which now resides with Ardys' sister, Phyllis.

Ardys loved her Indian experience and was anxiously looking forward to returning when she was just shy of age 15. With two weeks to go before leaving, Ardys noticed her parents weren't packing her belongings with everyone else's and asked why.

"They said 'We've decided you will stay here and go to high school in Upland,'" daughter Wanda recounted. "This made my mother feel abandoned. I think for years my mother could not express her anger at her parents or at God. Your parents are missionaries so you can't be angry with them because they are doing God's will. You can't be angry at God because then you're not a good Christian. She had grief issues that she was never able to explain because you can't be angry at God or your parents . . . I don't think she ever made peace with her parents about them leaving her. Her father lived until he was 102, but they were not close."

And who knows, perhaps the words of her Uncle Paul rang in her head, a reminder that she musn't keep her parents from their call.

"We were missionaries' children and God came first. We were there, but God came first. We didn't get the kind of parenting that children get. It did scar Ardys for life," said Marylou, who understood later that the Mission Board would not pay schooling or transportation for children once they reached age 16, a fact that could have played into her parents'

India for Christ
Rev. and Mrs. Charles Engle
Ardys, Marylou and Phyllis
Saharsa, Dist. Bhagalpur
India

decision not to take Ardys back to India. Ardys lived with her mother's cousin Hannah Foote and her husband, Alan.

In "My Story, My Song," Ardys writes, "I was left in the United States for educational and financial reasons. It was to be almost five years before I would see any of my immediate family again."

Perhaps to understand how the Engles could have left a child across the ocean, a story about their initial call to missions is in order. As Charles described it in his autobiography on file in the BIC Archives, he and his wife were at a BIC Conference in Fairland when the Home Mission Board made a call for workers: "My wife and I were in separate locations in the congregation and we both stood up. We hadn't planned or discussed it before and we both gave ourselves to the Home Mission Board." What would've happened had one and not the other stood up is a question worth pondering! When they were called in by the Board to discuss their call, they were accepted and asked when they would be ready to leave.

"I said, 'We're ready right now, tomorrow.' They looked at us and Bishop Engle said, 'Charles, don't you have your home back in California?' I said, 'We do, but it's on a foundation; it won't run away. We can leave here tonight if you want.' They were astounded," Charles wrote, but to him, forsaking all else for the sake of the Cross naturally included everything – even one's child, it would appear years later.

Left behind, Ardys finished high school and enrolled in Beulah College, which would later change its name to Upland College.

She stayed at the dorm at Beulah College one semester, and then stayed with missionaries Hannah and Alan Foote in their home. The next year, she found room and board as a helper for Dr. Arthur and Mrs. Weber. She answered the phone, cooked the morning and evening meals and did light housework on Saturdays, Marylou said.

"I knew Ardys before Alvan did. We were both students at Beulah College," boasted David Climenhaga, who would become bishop of the BIC church in Southern and Northern

Rhodesia from 1960 to 1965. He remembers both he and Ardys taught Sunday school classes at Alta Loma; she taught kids and he taught adults. A bunch of them would carpool together to the church and Ardys was the last stop.

"She always had some kind of very fragrant perfume and I would say, 'My Ardys, you smell nice!' She later told me that embarrassed her so much, but I think she liked it," he said with a chuckle.

In college, Ardys was a leader, serving as the first female president of the student body, something she was proud of even as an adult.

In 1942, the Engle females returned to the United States because the Japanese had invaded Burma and it was thought they might invade India next, Marylou said. In another surprise move, Marylou and Phyllis didn't know until they were boarding the ship that their daddy was staying behind.

Mrs. Weber suggested that Ardys meet her family privately at the train station – a stop before the nearest one in Ontario, Calif. The church would have a huge crowd of people waiting to greet the returning family; how thoughtful that the doctor's wife knew how much it would mean to Ardys to have a private reunion first. Mrs. Weber bought Ardys a train ticket and drove her to West Covina, to get on the train to meet her mother and sisters. "Ardys said it was a tearful and joyous reunion, and that Phyllis and I looked at her with big, unbelieving eyes," Marylou said.

Mrs. Engle and the girls came back to Upland, where Charles owned a home that they had rented out during the years they were gone. "The BIC church gave Mother $100 for the three of us for three months – that was $35 a month. In order to earn money, Mother had to rent out the extra bedroom. That meant Ardys couldn't move home with us. Once again, she was excluded. That hurt her a lot, but she understood," Marylou said.

"Ardys was only about 18 when we first came back from India, but she always seemed so much older to me. I was a little in awe of Ardys," said Phyllis, who was 10 at the time and didn't remember any of her life with Ardys in it at that point. "She came over a couple of times a week. She was very generous. I really looked up to her."

Phyllis and Marylou recall that they loved to go visit Ardys at the doctor's home on Euclid Avenue, a beautiful part of town.

"I remember we had really good meat there – lamb chops, roasts – things we couldn't afford. At age 12, my Saturday job was to bake coffee cake for the Webers," Phyllis said.

Ardys was already dating Alvan when her family returned from India. He was in medical school in Philadelphia. Her little sisters were fascinated with every detail of their long-distance romance. I remember he sent her a valentine that had cross sections of a spine split and dried to spell "Valentine." We thought that was so romantic! . . . The most wonderful thing anyone could have ever done!" Marylou said.

Upon her graduation from Upland College as a certified teacher, Ardys got a job in Pennsylvania, largely so she could be closer to Alvan. However, her mother got sick with a brain tumor and once again, Ardys sacrificed her personal dreams and comfort to serve another – this time, her mother and sisters. She returned to Upland in 1945 and taught there for the remainder of the school year. She even paid half the rent for the room she stayed in with roommate Sue Landis.

"When Mom had her first convulsion, it was Ardys who went with her in the ambulance to Los Angeles for testing. She was strong and we knew we could count on her," Marylou said. She remembers that, at the doctor's suggestion, Ardys got a room near the hospital.

"One day, Ardys was eating a sandwich at a nearby park and a man came up to her and said, 'Lady, you shouldn't be in this part of town alone. It's not a good place to be.' She was scared; she was only 21," Marylou said. As usual, however, she was putting others before herself.

Informed by cable that his wife was seriously ill, Charles returned from India the summer before his wife died in 1945. It had been three years since his family had seen him. Ardys returned to Philadelphia in August, but came dutifully home again in September at her father's request. Ardys was home when her mother died in November and for some months afterwards.

"After Mother became ill and died, Ardys was like a mom to us," Marylou said. "For Easter, she bought us beautiful dresses. Mine was yellow. I always felt so wonderful when I wore that dress."

Ardys often took her sisters shopping and bought them clothes. While their dad was against their modern dress, it was Ardys who told him that he needed to let them be young ladies and wear heels. Years later, it was Ardys again who stood up to Alvan on their daughters' need to dress fashionably and wear mini-skirts.

Ardys even had some advice for her grieving father, according to Marylou. "Instead of moping around, go back to school to complete your B.A." – and he did.

That next summer, on July 11, 1946, Alvan and Ardys were married in the Upland Brethren in Christ Church by Ardys' father.

Now her future was inextricably linked with that of an Ohio farm boy turned medical doctor.

In her last words to her father in her birthday essay, Ardys thanked him for his personal example of "putting God first in your life and serving others and witnessing for your Lord." It was an example she had tried to follow, she wrote, and added, "I'm sure at times I fail, but I keep persevering."

Her future with Alvan was going to take a special kind of perseverance that she would later acknowledge was the hardest yet most precious undertaking of her life.

During her college years, young Ardys had begun the serious pursuit of God's will her life. In "My Story, My Song," she wrote, "I realized that a complete surrender to personal ambition and goals was necessary. I also met Alvan Thuma, whom I later married."

One can't help but wonder if she ran those two sentences together on purpose.

----- 🕊 -----

Sena ulayanda kwangununwa sunu na?
Sena uyanda kumvwa kuumuna kwakwe?

Would you have Him make you free, and follow at His call?
Would you know the peace that comes by giving all?

Four
Would You Live for Jesus?

From her expansive front porch, Ardys Thuma could look across at the place that captured her husband's time and attention.

She could see the people passing on the dirt road in front of Macha Hospital – did she call any in? Probably not. It was a different time then. While blacks and whites greet each other easily here now and clasp hands, such was not the case before the war for independence. "I was afraid of white people," confessed Sarah Mwaanga, housekeeper for the Thumas for seven years, during which time she and Mrs. Thuma never had a personal conversation about their lives.

Across the street, her husband was asking all kinds of personal questions of his patients to gain their medical histories. It has been said that, at the bedside, Alvan became talkative, friendly and displayed compassion beyond the expected. His patients fell in love with him, revered him, thought of him as a god.

He never wanted for a friend.

In this atmosphere, Ardys, left to tend the house and garden, instructing girls 20 years her junior, fell silent.

"She didn't talk much," Sarah said. "I never knew her to have a friend." This was a description that flies in the face of everything Ardys normally was – talkative, a social butterfly.

There were of course other missionaries here, but Ardys, ever one to worry about what others thought of her, always judging herself too harshly and coming up short, did not form close friendships with them. Her gifts – teaching and hospitality – seemed to her not in high demand here.

61

Sometimes she caught Alvan's eye as he rushed in from the clinic to grab a banana or a handful of ever-present peanuts before heading off to the hospital and he smiled at her momentarily. It was still there, the spark that had drawn them together more than a decade earlier.

"Stay with me this afternoon!" she longed to say, but knew better. There was little privacy anyway, what with the house help always about and people constantly knocking at their door to ask for food or advice.

Ardys watched her husband stride across the dirt road toward the hospital and she felt such admiration welling up in her chest . . . this man, this husband of hers, was doing such wonderful things for God! It was her joy to support him in any way she could. His calling was her calling – and she didn't begrudge it one bit.

But sometimes, on days like today, when his smile was warm and meant only for her, Ardys fervently wished she could turn back the clock to the summer of 1946 when they were young newlyweds, crazy in love . . .

Ardys Engle met her future husband at Upland College, when he was a sophomore and she was a freshman.

Although Ardys' outgoing nature and love of parties, theater and culture would later seem the polar opposite of her husband, Ardys' sisters remember how outgoing Alvan was in the early years of dating.

"When Ardys first met him, he loved the theater and ballet. He took us to our first opera," Marylou recalled.

During the long hours of making and hauling bricks to build Macha Hospital, Alvan would regale the men with stories of his long-distance courtship – how he would hitchhike across the country to see Ardys.

"When she was going out with Alvan, we were so interested in the romantic parts of their romance," recalled little sister Phyllis with a chuckle. It was Ardys who gave Phyllis her much sought-after information about "the birds and the bees."

"I could tell Ardys all about my boyfriends and what was going on. Premarital sex was definitely not in the cards, but we still wanted to know about sex," Phyllis said.

She remembers that her new brother-in-law was in the first Kinsey Report. That is indeed true, Wanda confirms. Alvan, while a med student at Hahnemann, was one of the 5,300 men interviewed for "Sexual Behavior of the Human Male," which was published in 1948. According to the Kinsey Institute, the majority of the participants were young, white adults with some college education, referred to as "the college sample." Kinsey used in-depth, face-to-face interviews by highly-trained interviewers to question each participant on up to 521 items, depending on his/her specific experience (the average in each case being near 300). Histories covered social and economic data, physical and physiologic data, marital histories, sexual outlets, heterosexual histories and homosexual histories.

"Dad said he probably skewed the results since he was a virgin until marriage and hadn't done anything kinky," Wanda said with a chuckle.

If it's true that absence make the heart grow fonder, the hearts of Alvan and Ardys must have been full to overflowing because they didn't see each other for two years while she was in college in California and he was at Goshen College and later medical school in Philadelphia.

Finally, Alvan suggested that Ardys try to get a job teaching in Philadelphia, which she did and moved to be near him. That was, of course, cut short when Ardys returned to California to care for her dying mother. The next spring, Alvan went to California and proposed marriage at last.

"I do remember giving my mom a hassle for moving all the way to Philadelphia to teach, when Dad had not proposed marriage yet. I think her family thought she was taking a risk to move to Philadelphia to be near him, when he had not yet proposed. She said she was willing to take the chance as she thought this could be the man, and they would be near each other," daughter Barb said.

Perhaps one reason Ardys thought Alvan was Mr. Right was because of his call to missions. "I do know that my Mom always felt she would be a missionary, felt the 'call' and that was one thing they had in common, as Dad also felt he would be a medical missionary. I am aware of at least two other men my Mom dated in late high school and college and she said they did not feel called to be missionaries and thus their relationships did not continue," Barb said.

Alvan had never taken his sweetheart to meet his parents and siblings. He told them about his proposal of marriage in a letter dated March 7, 1946, "a beautiful Sunday morning" that saw Alvan rising at 7:30 a.m. even though he didn't intend to go to Sunday school, only church, he noted. Could his excitement over his wife-to-be have been the reason he couldn't sleep late?

"I really do have a purpose in writing you this morning; it is to give you the 'word' straight. When you hear it by the 'grapevine,' it would possibly be that we are married, but that is not so – we are only engaged to be married. I'm really sorry that I could not have brought her home for you to meet like as at Christmastime. I guess you'll just have to take my word concerning her."

Then, lest there be any doubt that level-headed Alvan could have made a brash move based solely on his hormones, he added, "May I say in closing, 'Love Is not blind;' reason and not reflex is still the controlling factor of our lives." Oh Alvan, could you gush a little over your sweetheart, please?

For six weeks after their July 1946 wedding, Alvan and Ardys lived in Sweet Home, Ore., where Alvan worked for a Mennonite logging company. The newlyweds lived in a one-room log cabin with no indoor plumbing other than one cold water tap. Ardys said later that this was a good introduction to the adjustments they would have to make later to life in Africa. The new bride cooked on a two-burner hot plate and heated water on it to use for laundry, which she did by hand. Yes, Sweet Home was surely a precursor to African life! The beautiful countryside made up for the sparse living conditions, Ardys said and besides, "We were young and in love!"

Ardys volunteered at the local hospital, where she got her introduction to the medical world. She was asked, but could not bring herself, to give injections to patients. She was no doubt glad to return to her teaching job in Philadelphia in the fall while Alvan finished his last year of medical school. She also worked part time at Strawbridge and Clothier.

Alvan and Ardys' first home in Sweet Home, Oregon

"Ardys loved dressing up and pretty clothes and jewelry – things we didn't have when we were growing up," her sister Phyllis said. "She loved matching purses and dresses. We all loved this. Ardys would've loved to learn to dance, I think."

After Alvan's graduation in the spring of 1947, the couple moved to Ohio, where Alvan interned at Miami Valley Hospital. Ardys worked at the hospital in the summer and got a teaching job in the Dayton School system in the fall.

Shortly thereafter, Ardys got pregnant and gave birth to son, Meryl, in August 1948. She gave up teaching. The following December, the Thumas moved to Souderton, Pa., where Alvan went into family practice with Dr. Paul Nase in January.

This Souderton home became "home away from home" for Phyllis, who was a senior at Messiah Academy. Marylou had married Orville Bert in 1948. "Alvan was interning on a modest salary, but he spared no expense in taking us out to eat, even for lobster tail!" Phyllis recalled. "Alvan wasn't particularly a gift giver at Christmas, but he'd send me a fruit cake in the middle of the year."

Ardys' (R) 2nd grade class at Ft Mckinley, OH 1947-48

Phyllis graduated in 1949; her father, remarried by this time to Kathryn Wingert, had left to go back to India in January of that year. He didn't come back for his youngest daughter's graduation. Phyllis shrugs at the memory, "It seemed like that's just how things were. You always knew God was first. It wasn't that different than a high-powered executive who always put his work first."

Phyllis, just 13 when her mother died, was eager for a new mother. So when Charles remarried in 1947, Phyllis had welcomed it. "For me, it was a godsend. I didn't have a mother or a boyfriend. Marylou had Orville. Ardys had Alvan. I was perfectly comfortable with calling her mother. My other sisters didn't feel the same way. She was much more aggressive than my mother," Phyllis said. "Ardys realized that Kathryn was very good for daddy, but to have her replace mother was very difficult for her."

Sixty-seven years after the remarriage, David Climenhaga, now in his early 90s, recalled with great clarity how Ardys had told him that her stepmother announced she was their mother now and they were not to talk of their own mother again. That Ardys would have related this detail to David and that he would have remembered it so clearly suggests it was no small detail to Ardys at all.

"My take on it was that Kathryn sort of wanted these girls to be her daughters and Ardys and likely Marylou weren't having any of that," said Elaine Thuma, Phil's wife. "It was hurtful to them that she got rid of their mother's things. Yet I never heard Ardys say anything negative about Kathryn."

Elaine had her own introduction to Kathryn's iron fist when she and Phil were on their way to Zambia and stopped in California. Kathryn had organized a missionary gathering and when they were ready to leave for it, Kathryn looked at Elaine's bare legs and instructed her that she could not go to the missionary meeting without wearing pantyhose. Elaine recalls that she "stomped" her way upstairs and put on hose. The two women got along fine after that. "I just needed to submit to the authority of Grandma and we were fine," Elaine said with a laugh.

When Kathryn landed at Messiah Village at the end of her life, it was Ardys who would be her prime caretaker. Once again, the gracious hostess and nurturer would put service to another above her own feelings – even service to one who had wounded her greatly years before.

"Certainly Ardys was the picture of love and compassion, very non-judgmental. She was a role model of dignity," said Phyllis, who, in 1952, married Royce Saltzman, a professor at Messiah and advisor to the yearbook when she was the editor. Phyllis taught special education and elementary school, something she and Ardys had in common.

After Alvan offered himself for missionary service and the idea of going to Africa became a reality, Ardys took the call as seriously as her husband.

In the April 1951 edition of the "The Evangelical Visitor," both Alvan and Ardys shared their feelings as they departed.

"What a privilege to hear the voice of God call and to follow after Him! What joy and peace comes to the hearts of those who are willing to surrender all to follow Him where He may lead," Ardys wrote, and then – hinting at the lack of self-esteem that seemed to characterize her opinion of herself – she wrote, "I feel most unworthy and yet greatly privileged to go as the church's and as Christ's ambassador to Africa."

Alvan wrote, "Last night at our little service aboard the boat, the statement was made, 'This is a sacred hour.' This immediately struck me, as truly this is a sacred hour for me. We were setting out a little like Abraham; setting out, not fully knowing but trusting in God."

Pausing to really think about what the Thumas were doing, it's easy to understand how magnificent yet terrifying that first night on the ship must have been for this young couple, a baby and toddler in tow, knowing they were following the call of God but knowing little else about what that meant. Alvan knew he was poised on a precipice that would change his life and the lives of those he hoped to serve. Change never comes without cost, he surely knew; and one can only imagine how much he pondered what that might be.

Alvan drew his strength from the One who called him, writing "We humbly go, knowing that there will be many problems and discouragements but also knowing that He in whose name we are going will give us strength and wisdom when needed."

Six months into their service at Mtshabezi, Ardys wrote "As the Doctor's Wife Sees It" – a glimpse of medical work at the hospital. Amidst the details of how the hospital looked and ran, Ardys wrote, "As I sit here and write this, I am made to think that missionary work isn't all teaching, preaching or even helping the sick, but it is a continuous living before these people the teaching of Christ. It is the way we raise our children; it is the way we treat those who work for us; it is the way we help them when they need help; it is the way we show our interest in their lives and their daily problems; it is the way we treat fellow missionaries; it is our very attitude toward life."

It is interesting to note that in this exhaustive list, one thing is missing – the way the husband and wife treat each other, which was surely on display for the house help, the fellow missionaries, the community people with whom the Thumas lived their lives.

Maybe it was just too personal to venture toward anything to do with the marital relationship in the pages of "The Evangelical Visitor," however, to those who lived and worked with the Thumas, it was obvious that their marriage was becoming background music to the more important business of medical and spiritual life on the mission field.

Their marriage continued to "play" in the background, a melody of notes strung together years before at the altar, but who was paying attention to the harmony?

"You had more to do than you should have had to do. Everybody was overloaded," said Keith Ulery, who would later become the mission superintendent at Sikalongo years after his 1-W service at Macha. "They were both strong personalities. Sometimes they clashed. I don't think they had much time together as a couple. They were both very busy. It was a good marriage with a lot of stress. Look, when my wife and I were missionaries in Sikalongo for four years, I bet we had less than five or six meals together with just Lucy and I and the kids. That was mission life."

Bob Worman, a surgeon who came to Macha in 1963 and worked alongside Alvan for about a year, was struck by the difference between Dr. Alvan, who demonstrated great compassion toward his patients, and Husband Alvan, who did not seem to extend that same warmth to his wife.

"It was sometimes hard to reckon the person he was with the Africans with the person he was with Ardys," he said. "He was almost two people."

Ardys was a talker and it often appeared that Alvan ignored her when she talked, he said.

"She could talk longer without taking a breath than anyone I knew," Bob, now 90, said, shaking his head.

"In his defense, he did shut down some of the time because she talked so much," his wife, Winnie Worman, 87, said.

"He wasn't a Romeo as far as I could observe. I never saw Alvan demonstrate any affection toward Ardys, but it wasn't done then and it was even frowned upon. I think he appreciated her, but it was an unspoken appreciation," said good friend Mim Stern.

The old adage says that "opposites attract," but maybe after some time together, they also repel. "They were different personalities," said Norma Steckley, a nurse who served at Macha with Alvan from 1957 to 1960. "She was very precise; he was more happy-go-lucky."

Alvan's laid back, easy-going demeanor – one reason why perhaps he didn't rush to sort the stacks of mail that built up on his desk and drove his wife crazy – irritated more than one woman on the compound.

"His famous saying was 'I don't go until my back is back against the wall' – meaning he doesn't plan ahead, he just responds to the needs," said Dorothy Gish, who taught at the Macha Girls School, now called Frances Davidson High School, from August 1958 to December 1964. "I think they just had such different personalities. She was very precise and organized and he was very laid back. She wanted to count on when he was going to Choma to get things she needed, but you couldn't pin him down. That frustrated all of us. I don't think he lived in the future, he lived in the present, at the moment. That attitude serves a missionary well and leaves you open to learning . . . . but it may not help your marriage."

Perhaps it was the circumstances at Macha that brought out the challenge in their marriage. Rich and Kathy Steubing, missionaries who credit the Thumas with acclimating them to Lusaka when they arrived in 1970, say they saw nothing of discord. In fact, to them, the marriage seemed complimentary. Both said that Alvan, who was then a medical officer at the University Teaching Hospital and a high ranking medical official in the country, supported Ardys in what she did with hospitality, which gave her a sense of purpose and fulfillment, and she supported Alvan in his work and greatly enjoyed the social connections that his high post brought to them.

"Days at Macha were just difficult, I think," Rich said. "We joke that Kathy would have died there!"

"It takes much more of your life as a woman in a rural mission station just to maintain yourself and your house. It's 99 percent the equivalent of washing dishes – you are making everything from scratch; if you want mayonnaise, you have to make it; if you want rolls, you have to make them; if you want tomato sauce, you have to make it," Kathy said."Then you have the pressure of things not working well – water and electricity. It's a lot of work just to live and sometimes there isn't much energy left over for anything else."

The Thuma siblings know their parents loved each other, but also recognize that their marriage suffered, in part because of the different needs and relational differences they brought to it but also perhaps because of the call from God that went before all else.

"From my viewpoint as a son, Dad was always approachable, when I was young and when I was older. He didn't demonstratively show his love, but I always felt loved. We didn't hug in our family, but I never sensed they didn't love me. We felt as a family that words are cheap and actions are more important. We just knew we loved each other. In her older years, Mom said 'I love you' more," said Phil, noting that even in his letters, his father signed them "as usual," not "love."

Phil certainly remembers wonderful times as a family, especially on vacation – away from the hospital – when they would take boat rides along the east coast of Africa to Tanzania, Kenya and Fishoek. "Mom and Dad were best of friends then. We had lots of fun together," Phil said. When they went home on furlough from 1957 to 1958, to New Madison, Ohio, he remembers no discord. Ardys took care of the children while Alvan got a job.

Upon returning to Macha after furlough, Ardys seemed completely happy. In the "Visitor" of December 1, 1958, she wrote that she did not feel the fear or excitement she felt when they first sailed for Africa. "This time, there is only the peace that comes from knowing that one is in the center of God's will and the joy of being in His service." That joy seemed to complete her as a missionary, mother and wife.

Thuma family holiday near Mombasa, Kenya

As a child, Phil recalls thinking his parents had a good relationship. "I never heard nasty words; they were always kind to each other." In adulthood, however, Phil remembers visiting his parents in Ohio after they returned from Africa and definitely noticing an edge between them. "Dad would be short with Mom," he said.

Barb remembers that her dad wasn't good at getting presents for her mother on her birthday or at Christmas. "He would say, 'Everything I have is hers.' 'Dad, that's not the point,' I'd say. He just didn't get it," she said.

Yet, she remembers as a child that she asked her dad, "Are you rich?" She tears up now as she recited his reply: "Yes, I'm rich. I have a wife and four children."

He didn't say he was rich because he had served the Lord or because he had started a great hospital or worked with a country in its independence; his riches lay in his family.

Ardys could have turned against this God who called her parents into service and away from her. Instead, she offered Him herself, her personal comfort and persevered through crude living conditions, tearfully sending her children away to boarding school, sharing her husband and always, always wrestling the depression that dogged her all her life . . . Why? For Christ. That others might see Him through her hospitality, through her husband's healing hands and through her son and grandson, whose love for the African soil runs as deep as that of her great-great Uncle Jesse Engle.

Alvan could have stayed in Ohio, no doubt been a successful farmer and/or doctor – his choice – yet he took God's gifts and used them in a foreign land to bring life and hope to thousands of people who looked nothing like him. Why? All because he believed that serving God was the utmost.

----- 🌍 -----

Maala wang' uuteleeli,
Ntiye nzube kwako.

Rock of Ages, cleft for me,
Let me hide myself in Thee.

Five
Rock of Ages

Martha Muleya stood at the stove, cooking what Mrs. Thuma always asked her to cook — beef and potatoes. By now, the African woman thought she should know how to cook this western food, but she always questioned whether the potatoes were cooked enough. Nshima was so much easier!

"Martha, how are you?" Dr. Thuma's soft-spoken words brought Martha out of her thoughts and into the kitchen, where her employer stood nearby.

"I'm fine, I'm fine, 'cept I was bit by a tetse fly and every time I sit down, I am tired!" the 23-year-old woman said. "I want to marry and have children some day, but I'll just fall on the ground with sleeping sickness."

"No, no. There is medicine for this," Dr. Thuma told her. "We will fix you up."

Martha smiled. She knew he would do his best. The Thumas had become her savior of sorts ever since she failed grade 9 and was faced with the reality of having to go back to her home village. That was until Elwood Hershey, superintendent of the BIC mission, promised to find her work if she would stay. That work was to cook for the new doctor in town.

Learning to cook for Americans was quite a trial for Martha, who snuck in ample helpings of a small root called "cuuwe" in hopes of drawing their taste buds over to her way of eating.

"Can you put me on your back?" asked little Phil, peering into her face with his large brown eyes.

"Can I put you on my back? Well, I'm cooking," she told the small boy. "Just wait." Later, Martha would say she carried Phil on her back,

an expression that means she cared for him, but she would insist she meant she literally carried him on her back along with a bowl full of cuuwe, his favorite food.

Mrs. Thuma was definitely the supervisor of the house, Martha knew. It was she who told the house help what to do and then made her rounds to make sure they were doing it. Martha was in the kitchen; there was also a server, a laundry person, a housecleaner, a dish washer and a gardener.

Mrs. Thuma loved people, Martha could see that right away. She loved talking with people and she loved helping people. When villagers knocked at her door, asking for food, Mrs. Thuma didn't hesitate to give what she could – even if it was something Martha was planning on cooking that night!

"You are very kind," she told Mrs. Thuma, but the doctor's wife just smiled and made an excuse for her generosity. She didn't know the language too well and it was easier to just be generous than try to explain why she couldn't.

In her spare time, Martha tried to teach Mrs. Thuma how to speak Tonga, but she never did learn too much of the tribal language. She wondered if this only added to Mrs. Thuma's apparent loneliness. Mrs. Thuma did not have a good friend, as far as Martha could tell.

"Martha, get me some water," Mrs. Thuma said many an afternoon in their early days together. Martha would dip cool water into a basin and take it to her employer, just in time for Dr. Thuma to walk in the door, sunburned from a day of digging at the hospital site.

Martha watched from the stove – where she often stood sentry – as Mrs. Thuma dipped fresh towels in the cool water and gently bathed the dust from her husband's reddened skin. Then she would dip the towel into the cool water again, wring it out and apply it as a cold compress onto his shoulders. The sight never ceased to amaze Martha; she wasn't used to seeing such tenderness on display.

Martha grew to love Dr. Thuma for his gentleness toward her people. Whenever someone would come to him with an illness or injury, he would inquire "Where are you hurt?" He would only have to touch whatever part of their body hurt and they would say, "I am fine." Martha had seen it herself. She never heard anyone complain if a loved one would die under Dr. Thuma's care because without him, they would have had no one to even try to save a life.

Martha came to have great respect for her employer and the feeling was mutual. Of everyone in the household staff, Dr. Thuma came to trust Martha the most.

One day he came to her, telling her that he and Mrs. Thuma would be going to a church meeting in Wanezi, Southern Rhodesia.

"Martha, when I look at you, my mind tells me that you are capable of doing whatever I ask you to do," he told her. "While we are gone, I want you to sleep here in our house and oversee things."

"I can't. I am a girl," Martha protested.

"You can," Dr. Thuma told her — and suddenly his confidence in her sprouted a healthy dose of her own self-confidence.

"On my own, I cannot but with the help of God, I can do it," she answered affirmatively.

"Now that you said that, I know you can do it," Dr. Thuma said.

He didn't tell Martha where the money was kept in the house. He and Mrs. Thuma left for Wanezi and Martha took her job seriously, telling the other staff what to do. When Dr. Thuma came back, he went at once and counted the money. It was the same amount he had left. He called all the girls who were working there and gave them an envelope of money because they had done well while he was gone. This was their bonus for work well done. Martha was given more money than the others because she was in charge.

Martha Muleya is 85 when she tells the story, but the pride still shines in her dark brown eyes, all these years later. Dr. Thuma believed in her and because of that, this young woman who flunked out of grade 9 finally began to believe in herself too.

"My faith in God is bigger than anything," declared Martha, who had nine children, only two of whom are still living.

A giant Tom turkey struts by, kicking up a little dust but not distracting Martha from the first order of business, singing praises. "Every promise in the Book is mine, every verse, every word, every line," she warbles in a high-pitched voice that still keeps a tune.

She married in 1958 and left the Thuma household, but she took with her many memories that remain in her heart. Today she lives next to the original clinic where Alvan first started practicing. She is stooped over when she walks, but her mind is sharp and strong.

"I knew Dr. Thuma very well," she declared. "Very well"

"Underline 'well,'" instructs her interpreter, Mutinta Nyirenda.

The number of people in the Macha community who knew Dr. Thuma personally is shrinking, but for those who remember him well enough to tell about him, it is obviously pure joy to remember him. Faces light up with wide smiles, eyes twinkle, minds search far back to pull up stories that bring delight in the retelling.

Aaron Chidakwa, headman of Chidakwa Village, now 79, recalls the impact that a visit to Dr. Thuma had on people.

"Back in the village, people would ask, 'Are you under Dr. Thuma?' and if the person said 'yes,' good, but people said if Dr. Thuma was not the one to see you, you might not get well because he was the best one," he said.

Bishop Thuma Hamukang'andu confirms, "There were very few cases that he failed to treat. That legacy is actually very strong."

The bishop relates similar stories: "We took someone who was very sick and Dr. Thuma just touched the patient and that patient got healed. People would say, 'He gave me an injection and I got well.' I asked Dr. Thuma about this once and he said it was actually water, but that people got 'healed' by God, not him. The old attitude was that if you didn't get an injection, you hadn't been seen."

Daniel Muchimba, headman of Mavu Village, first met Dr. Thuma when his wife was sick and he brought her to the dispensary at the BIC mission, in 1955. Alvan treated her because she had miscarried. Daniel remembers he was very kind in explaining what had happened.

In 1959, Daniel's wife was pregnant again and Daniel was in Mirimba on business; his wife was with him when she went into labor. He drove all the way from Mirimba to Macha – some 18 kilometers away – with his wife next to him, one of the baby's feet sticking out because his son was breech.

Alvan met them at the door of the hospital and escorted his wife to one of the rooms to deliver. "He pulled out the baby and said, 'Your wife is safe now.' She was all right. So he became my best friend at that time," said Daniel, now age 88.

And the child, like many in Macha and the surrounding area, was named Thuma because Daniel and his wife felt that Dr. Thuma saved his life. Today, Thuma Muleya, his son, works in the same halls as the man who saved his life; he is an ophthalmic assistant at Macha Hospital.

Doctors who worked with Alvan also have high praise for him.

"Alvan was the very best; a smart guy," said Dr. Harold Engle, who worked with him briefly when at Macha on short-term mission work. "He ran the show and he knew what to do."

Sitting at a lunch table in the memory-impaired unit of Messiah Village, where he would live until his death on December 20, 2013, Harold repeated the same things over and over, often things that had nothing to do with the Thumas. But every time Alvan's name was mentioned, he immediately said the same thing: "He was the very best."

Dr. Bob Worman, a former Navy flight surgeon, went to Macha in 1963, where he worked just one year with Alvan before the Thumas left Macha. Bob would remain for seven years.

"It was clear that he was very admired, but he didn't promote himself that way. He was a doer, in charge of everything at the hospital and beyond," Bob said.

When he arrived at Macha, Bob recalls his surprise at seeing that the hospital doctor was growing quite a few cornfields. "He was basically a farmer. He enjoyed the out of doors," Bob said. "We wondered where is this corn going to go? We didn't have anyone to sell it to. I think Alvan sold it and used the money for the hospital." Bob also marveled that Alvan could "do anything," from fixing the lawnmower to pulling the well pump when it didn't work.

Alvan commented on this reality in the Nov. 26, 1962 edition of the "Visitor": "Besides practicing medicine, I must maintain the place. I've seen the inside of the pump engine, the lorry diesel engine and the engine on the lighting plant, changed brushes on the generator and maintained two lawn mowers; I have fixed four flat tires and replaced a shaft in the lorry – all within the last three weeks." Add to that care of the 140 inpatients daily and the 174 outpatients and Alvan's days were more than full. Often he would be the one pronouncing a person dead and preaching at their funeral. "I keep stressing that the 'wood, hay and stubble' with which many are building will never stand and neither will the 'gold, silver, precious stone,' unless the foundation of our lives is Jesus Christ," Alvan wrote of his funeral messages.

Days were packed full and the doctors were never really off duty, Bob Worman recalled.

Alvan (L) with Bob Worman (R) and friend

"We would have rounds in the morning beginning at 8. I would take one ward (men's or women's) and Al would take the other. Each ward was one big room. After rounds, we would do outpatients. There would be a big long line of people waiting outside. We saw a couple hundred people a day," Bob said.

The people came on foot or on bikes from all the surrounding villages. Some of the people were very sick with malaria. Others had gastroenteritis, diarrhea, measles, TB, leprosy and more, Bob said.

His wife, Winnie, was a registered nurse and Bob's assistant, in addition to parenting their four children. The Wormans set up a simple operating room, which had no electricity; they did everything with lanterns. Winnie had a sterilizer – like a pressure cooker – that was powered by gasoline, with which to sterilize instruments and equipment. Prior to this, people were sent to Choma for surgery. Bob did C-sections, skin grafts and abdominal surgery.

"We never really closed for the day," Bob said. "We were out in the bush and out our window was the hospital so if somebody pulled up, you would see them and go to them."

Realizing that more nurses were needed to keep up with growing patient load, Alvan hoped to start a nurses' training school. There were only two or three trained missionary nurses at the hospital and "dressers," who were young girls that had finished seventh grade and worked at the hospital at night to give pills, change wound dressings and the like. In about 1957, Alvan opened a nursing school on the Macha campus. Soon after, however, the government said the school had not registered with the nursing council and shut it down, according to son Phil. The dream was not lost however; within a decade Macha Hospital did add a School of Nursing, which graduated its first class of nurses in 1969.

Money was tight for the missionaries and the hospital, Bob said, but Alvan didn't worry – he just figured he would grow more corn and sell it if need be.

Money was also very tight for the Africans who came for care. The prices were set for procedures to correspond to their meager incomes. In an article that appeared in an Ohio newspaper when the Thumas were home on furlough in 1958, Alvan shared that a baby delivery was the most expensive procedure, at 75 cents. A case of pneumonia, including hospitalization and medication, was set at about 40 cents.

In the same story, Alvan shared his initial reaction at arriving at Macha: "When we first saw the facilities the natives had, we were astounded. A series of mud and pole huts served as the hospital, with another couple of huts as their living quarters."

Glenn Schwartz, a 1-W worker, remembers that Alvan told him he that he could look in a child's mouth and tell if he was going to graduate from secondary school. At the primary school, Alvan would look in mouths and tell the children's nutrition level by their teeth. Good nutrition equals good teeth equals "will graduate," Alvan told Glenn.

He also remembers that Alvan had an unusual way of deciding if a pregnant woman was having a girl or a boy – "And he was never wrong."

"If a woman asked him, 'Am I going to have a boy or a girl?' he would say, 'You're going to have a boy' and then, in his date book, he'd write 'girl.' When the baby was born and it was a boy, he'd say 'Didn't I tell you you were having a boy?' or if it was a girl, he'd say 'I have it right here in my date book – girl,'" Glenn said, laughing as he told the story. "He had a good sense of humor and he loved that hospital. He did everything from administration to the building to PR to grant writing."

Alvan's care extended past the patients to the missionaries, over whom he apparently felt some responsibility to keep watch.

Alvan delivered the Kiblers' second and third babies at Choma Hospital. In the early 1960s, the missionary wives went to Choma to deliver because it was considered better than Macha at that time, former mission superintendent George Kibler said. When their third daughter was ready to come, Alvan got in the car with the Kiblers in order to deliver her in Choma. Ever prepared, Alvan took a shovel along in case the expectant party would get stuck.

One time, George cut the tendon in his finger while in Sikalongo and got in his car and drove 60 miles to Macha in order for Dr. Al to sew up his hand.

Norma Steckley relates a story where "his heart of compassion really came through."

A carload of ladies had gone from Macha to Livingstone and were on the way home during the rainy season. "We got to a stream that was flooded and we couldn't get the rest of the way back to Macha. There was a little store that happened to have a phone and we called Al to tell him we were OK. Alvan had told us that he wasn't going to worry about us, but he answered on the first ring – at midnight!" she said.

Alvan also cared about the Zambian staff. Daughter Barb recalls when there was a single mother, a nurse, who again got pregnant. "There was talk that she should resign because it wasn't right, being pregnant with no husband, but Dad said no, she should stay because she needs her job and she's a good nurse," Barb recalled.

Perhaps no one worked harder than Alvan asked himself to work.

"I remember him with his old helmet with a bandana under the helmet and it was wet with sweat – that's how hard he worked. He worked right alongside the guys," Mim Stern recalled.

Wanda remembers her dad literally lying on the floor trying to get a nap because he was up delivering babies the night before.

Dorothy Gish, Macha Girls School teacher, also witnessed the effect that overwork took on Alvan.

"He and George Kibler would take turns preaching. One time, George said, 'Brother Thuma will lead us in prayer' and when nothing was said, he turned around and saw that Al was asleep. He probably had been up all night and was just exhausted," she said.

Stephen Muleya, a teacher at Sikalongo for most of his life except 1958 when he taught a year at Macha Central, marveled at the doctor's energy. "You couldn't know he was a doctor because he would join in the hard work with a wheelbarrow to help build the hospital," he said.

Now age 82 and living in Choma with his wife, Rosa Kababa, Stephen remembers, "He was a man of few words and more to do."

His wife, who said she was asked to be the first nursing student at Macha, later worked as a nurse at Macha Hospital under Alvan. "He was always very busy. He was always very kind, not fierce," she said, adding that she was not afraid of him as "The doctor."

On holiday, July 15, 1954, a couple of months before the move to Macha, Alvan writes to friend and missionary nurse Rhoda Lenhert, giving insight on his state of mind – tired!

"Possibly you wonder why we are traveling as we were to be missionaries in Africa. After three or four years in the field, one is given a holiday of three months to be spent away from the Mission, preferably at the Coast. Some of our older missionaries thought it was the altitude that had troubled them or the chronic malaria. Today some said it is the heat, or the tropical anemia or low blood pressures, that wears one down in the mission field. For me, it is none of the above, but the daily problems that keep taxing one to capacity. The 'struggle for survival' is basic and one feels it in all ways; physically, mentally and spiritually. Yes, short holiday is a welcome time."

Alvan carried another title besides that of "Doctor" – he was also an ordained minister with the Brethren in Christ. It was the practice in those days to ordain all male missionaries. This meant that Alvan always had to wear a clerical collar when he went to church or even on certain official business trips. Alvan never liked that collar.

Church leaders in Africa – Alvan (center, back row) with clerical collar

"As children, we remember him complaining a lot about having to wear it. When he was sent to Macha, the rule of the time was that all ordained ministers had to sit on the platform every Sunday with their clerical collars on.

Dad rebelled against the practice after some time and stopped wearing a collar. His excuse was that he had been too busy at the hospital on Sunday morning to go home before church and change into a collar, so the missionary in charge of the mission told him he could no longer sit on the platform. And thus Dad got his way, and was 'allowed' to sit down in the audience wearing a regular shirt, which was what he really wanted to be doing in the first place!" Phil said. "Interestingly, in his old age, he was proud to show everyone that he was an ordained minister in the BIC church, and Wanda kept his membership dues (or credentials) paid and up to date until he died."

Wanda confirmed this and said that she would ask her dad if he wanted to renew his license and even from the nursing unit at Messiah Village, he did. When the new papers came, he would put them in a drawer by his bed and that was that.

When it came to evangelizing, Alvan preferred to teach by action rather than by preaching. Sermon notes left behind in his small black binder emphasize the need for Christians to be a light in whom others may see Christ. "The best way to witness and grow is to live Christ-like lives . . . our actions speak louder than words," he wrote, then quoted Matthew 5:16 "Let your light so shine before men that they may see your good works and glorify your Father who is in heaven."

Likely Alvan would have agreed with Dr. John Spurrier's philosophy of missions: "God gifts people in the Kingdom of God in different ways. We have a holistic view – that God is interested in our minds and our bodies. We think good research and making people well makes God happy as much as preaching to them about Jesus."

As busy as Alvan was doctoring, building, preaching, visiting, problem solving and generally acting as the go-to person for just about anything, Ardys had her hands full overseeing a household bustling with hired help, young nurses and missionaries, 1- Ws, visitors and, eventually, four children.

Ardys ran a welcoming and well-structured home. Perhaps in the face of everything new and different, setting up a smooth-running household gave her familiar footing on which to land.

Ardys, a teacher by training, spent much of her time overseeing the tasks of the large household staff, planning meals and home schooling whichever children of hers were not yet age 6 and off to boarding school. Many of the nurses, 1-Ws and sometimes young missionaries ate with the Thuma family. She worked with a wood-fired stove, a kerosene refrigerator and lantern lights but thankfully she had indoor plumbing and a good water supply. She enjoyed making wedding dresses and cakes for the house help, no doubt lending a western flair to African celebrations.

"Her hospitality really shone there. Her home was always open. She was a very good cook," said Edith Miller, who was an educator at Macha from 1957 to 1982, serving as the first principal of the Macha Secondary School for Girls in 1965. "She was active with women in the church at Macha, leading Bible studies and prayers."

"Ardys was a very sociable person. She was like my mom when I was there. She cooked and did my laundry," recalled Joe Ginder, a 1-W at Macha. "She was very kind to the Africans. They would come to the door, asking for things and many missionaries would get upset, but she would always pay attention to them and was very sensitive to what they needed. She was inclined to give them what she could, more so than other missionaries."

In a letter to Alvan's parents in 1963, Ardys wrote about her busy life, mentioning how she had evening prayers with the hospital staff, led a Bible club once a week for all the missionary children, taught a weekly Sunday school class and played the organ for junior church and sometimes adult church.

In her letters, Ardys expressed shame for not keeping in better touch with people at home, but her life seemed a whirlwind of entertaining guests, cooking, mending and housework.

Alvan's schedule, as she described it in her letters, was even busier. She liked to share a running list of what conditions he had treated that week – anything from c-sections to extracting a fish hook from a man's hand to picking up sick patients along the road and a planned hernia operation that didn't happen because "the patient ran away." In between all this activity, Ardys described her busy day in the kitchen, making supper for arriving guests – which featured bologna brought from the States, boiled monkey nuts, cheese, corn on the cob, Chinese cabbage, mango chutney and bananas, oranges, berrie and passion fruit, "all grown here of course." The main dish was pheasant pot pie – "Alvan shot the pheasant" is noted in parenthesis! (Add hunter to the list of Alvan's capabilities. Though not an avid hunter, he taught his boys to shoot and took them on a two-day hunting trip when Meryl turned 16.)

At one point in June of 1964, Alvan was caring for patients at Choma Hospital as well as Macha, while the Choma doctor was on holiday. During those six weeks, he did 71 operations at Choma Hospital, Ardys noted. These were easily 12-hour days or longer. And what did he plan to do with the extra money he made for working so hard at Choma? Buy himself something new? No, he earmarked the money to get more water supply at Macha . . . "Perhaps get another bore hole dug because this season, we have not had enough to have a garden during the dry season," he said.

In many ways, Ardys seemed to take things in stride, "It appears Meryl may be getting chicken pox. Isn't that delightful? Ha!" she wrote home from Mtshabezi in a letter from April 1954. In the same letter, she gave the reader a taste of life in Africa: "We are expecting a policeman for dinner. I killed two chickens Friday as we're having one tonight. I finished my nylon dress yesterday. It really is a dream."

She also seemed remarkably happy to do without the things that in America were standard fare. "I'm really anxious to see (my stroller), but I certainly don't feel deserving of all these new things! Ha!" she wrote home in the same April 1954 letter.

Even before she left America, she was already content for the few things she would be taking along and hesitant in her suggestions for more. In a December 1950 letter to good friend Mary Lenhert, she wrote an answer to the Pleasant Hill Sewing Circle about what more they could make for them in addition to the 18 scrub suits, four dresses for Ardys and several slips and overalls for children.

"Alvan thought he should have some small towels like you would use in surgery, also to cover trays, etc. He thought maybe three or four dozen. What do you think? We priced material here at 32 cents a yard. They would be very simple to make; just two hems to stitch on the machine."

An account of their third Christmas in Africa, in December 1953, given by Ardys in the March 1954 "Visitor" makes clear just how much she treasured her role as hostess.

"December 19th began our pre-Christmas festivities; it was also my husband's birthday so I baked an angel food cake for him (With cake mix sent from the States.) . . . We were expecting (other company) for dinner. I had made chicken and homemade noodles, had string beans from the garden, and a Jello salad. I had helped make some refrigerator Kool-Aid ice cream." (Whatever that is, Ardys made it a lot!)

Two days later, she was busy making food for the Missionary Christmas Picnic – fried chicken, cookies, macaroni salad and roasted peanuts. In the midst of this, she cheerfully related that she was doing laundry and having "a little difficulty" because Alvan was installing a new wash line using steel posts instead of wooden ones, which had been eaten away by white ants. Her interim washline apparently wasn't strong enough so her sheets and other clothes fell down and she had to rewash them – no small task the first time, let alone a second time!

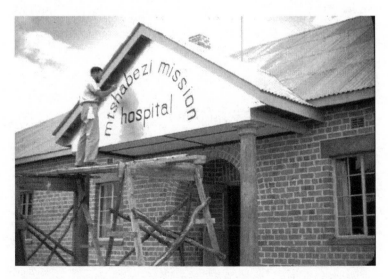

Alvan painting the sign at Mtshabezi Hospital

After a successful Christmas picnic at an outschool between Mtshazbezi and Matopo – complete with Phil and Meryl singing songs and doing recitations they had long practiced for the Christmas program, Ardys began to decorate her house for Christmas, although she notes it was much too hot to feel like Christmas to her!

On December 23, the missionaries caroled in Sindebele and English to the hospital patients, which Ardys thoroughly enjoyed. Christmas Eve day was spent entertaining the African nurses and "two young Christian men from Bulawayo" who came for the weekend. Christmas morning dawned early with strains of "Joy to the World" sung by African girls who were caroling to the missionaries. After Phil and Meryl opened their presents, Alvan and the nurses headed to the hospital while Ardys began to make food – lima beans, candied sweet potatoes and salad – for Christmas dinner at the main mission house.

Church was next. "It was very, very hot as we walked to the church, but since this was my third Christmas in Africa, it seemed quite natural for it to be blistering hot on Christmas day," she wrote. "How wonderful to worship the Lord on His birthday, whether it be in a church with thatch roof and mud floor or a church with beautiful steeple, stained glass windows and carpet-covered floor."

After a day that featured fellowship and more Kool-Aid ice cream and evening prayer, Ardys and her family left the main mission house for their own house.

"As we drove towards our home and I saw the outline of the hospital ahead of us – for the sun was fast sinking in the west – I thanked God that I had had the privilege of celebrating a third Christmas in Africa and prayed that if it be His will, I might have the happy privilege of celebrating many, many more Christmases in Africa," she said.

It would be their last in Mtshabezi. The following summer, they were sent to Macha.

"We came in October, the worst month to come – so hot!" Phil recalled.

Phil has many memories of playing with puppies, watching crews dig the ground for the hospital and playing around the perimeter. He recalls his father witching for water, planting the mango trees behind the hospital and coming up with the idea for "the fires" – the area behind the hospital where family members would camp out while their loved ones were patients. His mother, he recalled, ran the household, cooking everything from scratch, tending the big garden, pasteurizing the milk. It was Phil's job to churn it into butter.

Other missionaries have warm memories of the Thuma children as well.

"Meryl was quite an explorer. He started to raise some silk worms. I always wondered what happened to those," said Norma Steckley.

Edith Miller, who lived a mile from the Thumas and enjoyed many a meal at their home and many an hour in the car with them, laughs as she recalls the time that a bunch of them were driving down the road when Phil opened the car door suddenly. Alvan reprimanded him, but the small tyke said he "just wanted to see if the wheels were going around!"

She also remembers this story about Barb, who was about age 4 at the time: The smallest Thuma was leaning her head down over and a long string of mucus was hanging from her nose. Ardys asked her what on earth she was doing and she said, "I'm having an experiment to see how long it will get!" Edith found this hysterically funny. "Her father was a doctor. She was interested in experiments too," she said.

Former Macha Central teacher Stephen Muleya remembers how beloved the Thuma boys were, but he saw a difference: "Meryl was highly loved by the mother; Philip was most loved by the father," he said. How does he know this? "When the boys were working in the garden, the mother sneaked food to Meryl, not Philip," he explained somberly then brightened. "Those sons worked like Zambian boys; they really worked hard."

Ardys arrived in Africa with two small boys in tow; while there, she would give birth to two girls, Wanda on January 22, 1955 and Barb on July 3, 1957.

When she was pregnant with Wanda, Ardys was teaching at the teacher training school at Macha. Jacob Muchimba, a boy from Sikilongo was her student. "Mrs. Ardys was a very good teacher. She was very good because she never punished me!" he said.

He was present for the infamous incident when Ardys fainted at school while pregnant with Wanda.

"She sat on the chair and she fainted! We tried to revive her. We threw a bucket of water on her. That water was cold and it brought life back!" he said with a laugh.

Jacob Muchimba conversing with author

Jacob, who says he was born sometime between 1932 and 1936, went on to become a teacher himself in Choma and credits Ardys with modeling how to be a good teacher. He is blind now due to glaucoma and can't see to read or write anymore, which causes him great sadness. He smiles and asks after Wanda, the baby who wasn't born that day so long ago.

The women who worked at the Thuma house still recall that Dr. Thuma told everyone that he would ring the bell outside the mission if it were a girl. In the middle of the night, the clear sound of a bell pealed. Mutinta (the Tonga word used when a newborn child of the opposite sex of its siblings is born) was here!

"Dr. Thuma rang a bell to say Wanda was born. Woo! We ran when we woke up in the morning to see Wanda!" recalls Martha Muleya, pointing at the very tree that still stands from which the bell hung.

Alvan wrote of Wanda's birth in a letter to friends Dr. Paul and Mary Lenhert on Jan. 24, 1955: "The delivery took place here in our house. We had prepared for a delivery most any place in the past two weeks, Ardys and I traveled about 680 miles over roads of various descriptions, mostly bad. I no longer believe that rough roads will throw a woman into labor.

Ardys had varying degrees of contractions all day on Saturday . . . the baby was born at 9:55 p.m. Central African Time. It was a normal delivery in all ways and the baby looks very much like Meryl did. Not much hair, a round face, small ears and nose, a very nice looking baby, I'm sure you all would agree."

Then – enough of that baby talk – Alvan was back to medicine as he wrote in the next paragraph, "The Executive Board approved all the plans we presented to them so now I must take them to the government Department of Medicine . . . "

Here's a picture of life with the addition of a third child, gleaned from a letter that Ardys wrote to the Lenherts on March 18, 1955:

"This is Tuesday and this week has already proved busy. Sunday our revival began. I haven't been able to attend the services as much as I would have liked to, because of having a seven- week-old girl, but often I go in the evenings and Alvan goes to the noon day services . . . We don't like to take the children at night because the mosquitoes are so bad, and malaria is so plentiful here in Northern Rhodesia. We adults always wrap something around our legs so as to keep the mosquitoes off our legs, at least.

"Yesterday was one of my bread making days. I usually bake twice a week. I also made rolls for lunch and some coffee cake for breakfast. Our eggs are scarce these days and sometimes I hardly know what to fix for breakfast. We have pancakes a lot. We always eat a pretty heavy breakfast, for we need it for the work which lies ahead.

"Alvan and Edna have been seeing around 120 outpatients every day now for some weeks, besides taking care of the 55 inpatients we have. This morning there was a death of a child, a funeral, a small operation, plus seeing outpatients and patients so the medical work continues to go forward. Our cry is more room to put the patients and more time to get some building done.

"Yesterday I planted some peas in my garden. This afternoon I had to set out some lettuce plants, but it rained instead and so kept me from it . . . I am pleased with the way Meryl is doing in his school work . . .Philip has been occupied most of the day with a little bird that is crippled. He is trying to feed it and keep it alive. He calls it his little baby."

Many missionary mothers and farmers' wives would home school for Kindergarten and first grade then send their children off to boarding school at age 6. Youngways Hostel was set up for BIC missionary kids from Zimbabwe and Zambia missions – about 20 kids then. Mim and Pete Stern were houseparents there from 1960 to 1972. They had three of the four Thuma siblings and saw Meryl through to his departure for college in the U.S.

"Wanda was special – she was one you could always count on to participate," Mim recalled. "One time she got up to read her composition and she read each of the characters with different accents, one with a British accent, one with an American accent . . . it was so funny!"

Meryl was "the whip," Mim recalled – the oldest child there and the one who pulled things into line and got the kids up at 6 a.m. by playing the piano. Phil was a good boy, much quieter than Meryl, but "loyal as anything," she recalled.

The Thumas used the experience of boarding school as a time to instill confidence in their children. While other missionaries usually gave the keys to their children's trunks (which contained all their belongings) to the adult missionary chaperone on the train, Alvan and Ardys handed the keys to their children and told each that they were responsible for keeping it safely.

"That's an illustration of how our parents showed faith in us," Phil said. "That small act helped to build our self esteem and made us feel trusted by our parents, even though we may not have deserved it! I maintain that little things like that can shape a person's future personality – and their future level of self-confidence – more than we might realize."

The Thumas kept a stiff upper lip when sending their children away for months at a time. For Ardys, it probably took all the strength she could muster to do it with a smile.

Phil (L), Meryl (Ctr) and Wanda (R) on train to school

"I don't know if it was my mother's preparation or that we are fairly independent, but I don't remember any of us crying that we were leaving Mom," Wanda recalled. "My older brothers had forged the way. I think it comes down to what you script for your children. My mother never got upset or cried. I remember she would check things off a list as we packed and she made it seem exciting that we were going. She later said she cried when she got home, but she wasn't going to set us up to cry by crying in front of us."

Two years later, the youngest child of Alvan and Ardys – Barbara – was born.

That's a story Keith Ulery tells that matches the best of any Alvan Thuma story:

"Doc had to go to Lusaka for a medical conference. He was sure Ardys wouldn't deliver while he was gone. Well, she went into labor and called me to drive her to Choma," Keith said. "Part way there, her water broke."

Keith had to pull over and help dry her off, sticking a towel between her legs. "She kept saying how embarrassing it was and I told her, 'Well, I'll just be the Doc here.' We made it the rest of the way and when we got there, I just beeped the horn and they came running out. They all knew the Thumas. Every time Ardys saw me after that, she'd say something about how I helped deliver her baby."

Wanda and Barbara at Macha

Barbara has wonderful memories of growing up at Macha, where people of varied tribes and nations were regular visitors to her home. Her father, though busy, was attentive to her and loving, she recalled. She would often ride along to Choma when she was 5 or 6 and wait in the car while her dad helped a European doctor there do surgery. Although these were work-related outings for Alvan, for Barbara, they were special daddy-daughter dates where she could gain all of Alvan's attention on the hour or longer ride to and from Choma on a bumpy, gravel road. On a daily basis, she doesn't recall spending much time with her dad, but on vacation, he would make a conscious effort to plan fun outings with them.

The women who worked at the Thuma house have memories that are vivid, more than 50 years later.

Sarah Mwaanga worked for the Thumas starting at age 19. The Lord Himself sent Sarah to talk with Mrs. Thuma, the 76-year-old Zambian woman insists.

She was 19, a local school girl having trouble with math when she met Mrs. Thuma.

"I began to think, 'How can I pass math?'" Sarah recalled as she sat in her humble home in the village of Mizinga, close to Macha. She remembers going to see Mrs. Thuma and telling her about her trouble with math. She got up all her courage and asked, if she failed math, could she come and work for Mrs. Thuma? The answer was "yes" and, when indeed Sarah did fail math, she went to work in the Thuma household. All the missionaries had house help; it was the custom and it provided income for the local people.

"I didn't know how to do the work, but Mrs. Thuma explained it very well," Sarah said with a laugh. She was one of three people who worked at the house at that time. Her duties were to wash dishes and sweep the house. She started out working at the old house and moved up to the new house with the Thumas.

"I was the one who kept all the bedrooms clean. I made Dr. Thuma's stacks of books look nice," she said referring the piles that drove Ardys crazy. For her part, Sarah denied that her employer was messy. In this culture, it would be impolite to say if he were.

The pay was small and sometimes the Thumas gave her vegetables from the garden to supplement the pay. She worked for the Thumas for six years, until she got married in 1961.

"They became an important family to me when I failed mathematics," Sarah said. "The Lord led me to go see Mrs. Thuma . . . People still talk about Dr. Thuma --- he was a good doctor; he was a humble man."

Sarah became just as important to the Thumas. She worked for Phil Thuma's family when they later lived at Macha. "Phil is quiet like his father. Even his appearance reminds me of Dr. Thuma. When you look at Phil, you can't miss where he comes from," Sarah said.

She also worked for Dr. John Spurrier's family, doing laundry, cooking, cleaning and helping Esther Spurrier learn Tonga. Today, she is still a treasured friend of both families.

Sarah Mwaanga (L) and her daughter, Moono

When Dr. Spurrier's son, Matthew, married in December 2002, Sarah made the trip from Macha to Pennsylvania to attend the wedding – her first trip outside of Zambia.

"She was fascinated by the snow. She would walk outside to feel it," Esther remembers. "Sarah also marveled that one never saw people walking around outside their houses. In Zambia, village people live outside and only sleep in their houses."

Sarah found the Pennsylvania weather to be on the cold side She started to wear slacks for warmth and decided to wear them home to her village to show her daughters how modern she had become!

Esther Mwaanga, better known as Bina Ezra, was born in 1930 and lived most of her life in Bulebo, a village five or six kilometers from Macha Hospital.

When the Thumas arrived, she recalled "I am the one who said 'welcome.'" She worked in the garden most and was one of 10 who worked there.

Weak and recovering from pneumonia and congestive heart failure in the summer of 2013, she remembered life in the Thuma household.

"Mrs. Thuma didn't like to talk too much. She would tell the workers what to do," she said. "Mr. Thuma was a gentle man, a good man . . . He used to talk to the workers . . . when he was preaching, he had a very nice voice . . . . My, my, my, he was a good man. . . . He was humble. That's what made him special."

Bina Ezra especially loved the Thuma children. She took them to gather wild vegetables ('relish') out in the bush and remembered that they "helped very well."

As for Barbara, Bina Ezra remembered how she would carry all her stuffed animals on her back.

At the mention of Mutinta (Wanda), Bina Ezra put her thumb to her mouth . . . yes, Wanda sucked her thumb. "She was quiet and respectful," Bina Ezra said.

These beloved African women were the ones to see the Thuma marriage and family up close, ever-present ears and eyes in every room of the house.

"Ardys would laugh with us. Dr. Thuma and Mrs. Thuma would laugh together. The boys were good," Bina Ezra said. "Dr. Thuma didn't talk very much. He didn't make chatter and even the wife, she didn't talk a lot."

Ardys enjoyed reading and tending the garden, the former housekeepers recalled. Martha Muleya cooked the meals and Sarah served them, but she didn't eat with them. All the single missionary women would eat at the Thuma table.

Did Sarah and Mrs. Thuma talk? No. "I wouldn't talk to her about my life or my problems because I was scared of white people," Sarah said. She remembers that Ardys would often be writing letters; and she didn't go out visiting people very much. She wasn't one to chat with the help about her life or her family. Sarah remembers that many people – blacks and whites – came to the house, but she doesn't know why.

Did Mrs. Thuma have a friend? "I didn't see that," she said.

Martha declares that she never saw either Dr. Thuma or Mrs. Thuma upset and that the children "always listened." Her interpreter laughs and tells her that we also want to hear the bad, but Martha just shakes her head and says she remembers nothing amiss in the Thuma household.

Others, however, did notice something wrong . . . almost everyone saw it, but even today, few will talk about it unless prodded.

Ardys Thuma suffered from clinical depression, the likes of which could send her to bed for days.

"I think a lot of the depression was that she would compare herself to others and come up short," said Mim Stern, echoing the words of several people who guessed at the cause of Ardys' unhappiness. "I knew she had depression and sometimes she would comment that she felt worthless. In those days, we didn't talk about those deep feelings."

"Oh yes, I saw her depression. I knew she spent a lot of time in bed," said former mission superintendent George Kibler. "In general, she stayed close to the house and only associated in a limited way with other missionaries."

George remembers one instance where the women were getting together to make potato chips and they didn't invite

Ardys. When she found out later, George said she voiced her dissatisfaction at not being included.

"I think because of her illness and her complaints, you just kind of pushed friendship away. . . .You didn't seek Ardys out as a confidante or as someone to have fun with," he said.

Yet Mim, whose husband was mission superintendent from 1955 to 1959, has many fond memories of holding African teas with Ardys, usually at the Thuma home. Ardys was always ready to take her share of the work and, as countless others attest, Ardys was a welcoming and solicitous hostess.

Perhaps Ardys felt somewhat sidelined by her husband's enormous shadow. "She had a bit of an issue with Al getting all the glory and she was just his wife. She would shed many tears over this." Mim Stern would tell me and say, "What can we do to help Ardys?" I knew she had an emotional problem; I wouldn't have called it depression. I'd say she was insecure," offered Joe Ginder, who spent a lot of time at the Thuma home when he was in 1-W Service from 1954 through 1957.

"She was a 'feely' person. There were times when I saw her cry over things she couldn't control. She exuded the impression of being easy going, grin and bear it, just swallow it and move along, but I think she minded things more than she let on," said Keith Ulery, who saw the Thumas up close and personal. "She wasn't even-keeled, but people loved her."

Ron Herr, son of Alvan's sister's Mary, said he heard later that Ardys would be in bed for depression, but if guests would arrive, she would rise up out of bed and be congenial. "She had a strength to rise above her circumstances and do what was expected of her and represent her family well," he said.

"Ardys had a class about her . . . in her style and her appearance," said Ron's wife, Erma – and not even depression could take that from her.

For daughter-in-law Elaine, who would see her mother-in-law's depression firsthand in later years, knowing how to respond was daunting. Depression was something with which Elaine had no experience.

"Dad would say, 'She's not feeling well.' There would be times when she would be in the bedroom and we wouldn't see her for hours. When she got herself together, she would come out of the bedroom and interact. I never knew what set off her depression. It was just an awkward feeling. I could sometimes hear her crying," Elaine said.

As the wife of a missionary doctor as well, however, Elaine said she could see where Ardys might feel "back-burnered" at times.

"I experienced that myself sometimes, like when we filled in for Phil's dad that year that they returned to Macha," she said, referring to 1975 when Alvan spent a year working at Macha Hospital and left son Phil to cover his practice in Ohio. "People called Phil whenever, never mind that we had a three-month-old screaming baby and we hadn't seen him for days. Phil stepped into big expectations of what a doctor will do anytime of the day or night. This was a small town practice. Dad would never say no. For me, it was a year; for Mom, it was a lifetime."

At his mother's funeral, Phil was determined that his mother's struggle with depression would be talked about because, he reasoned, it would be mentioned if she had suffered with cancer or any other medical condition. Talking about it would hopefully take away some of the stigma associated with mental health issues, he hoped.

The revelation didn't sit too well with some family members.

"Her children called it depression; I never heard anything about it before they mentioned it at her funeral," said her sister Marylou. However, she went on to say, "In her later years, she would call me, often upset. She thought she was not liked by people. I know she felt Al was more interested in his work than in doing things with her, after they came back to Ohio."

Her younger sister Phyllis doesn't discount her oldest sister's discontent, but "to hear of her lying in bed with depression doesn't go with the picture I have of her being so involved in life," she said.

Phyllis wonders if the challenging circumstances of life at Macha contributed to her sister's depression. "Life was difficult for her there. She was maybe not as appreciated by Alvan. She felt that she really always wanted to be with people and Al was a loner. He was a people person as far as his work was concerned and people loved him for that," she said.

However others, like Dorothy Gish, said Ardys didn't seem to dislike being at Macha – and indeed Ardys' own words written in letters home and in the "Evangelical Visitor" indicated her delight at living in Africa. "From her comments, I got the idea that Alvan never really lived up to her expectations. I think she was disappointed," Dorothy said.

When Winnie Worman tried to talk to Ardys about her depression, all Ardys would say was that she was "sad."

"She felt inferior," said Edith Miller, now age 79.

Around the dinner table, populated by young, single nurses who took their meals with the Thumas, medicine was often the topic of discussion and Ardys watched her reserved husband come alive as he talked shop with the nurses. There she sat, feeling left out and maybe even threatened.

"Looking at it from her perspective, her husband was a doctor, helping people and highly regarded. And what was she doing? I think she always envied the teachers and nurses because they had something to do," Dorothy said.

Although Ardys had much to be proud of, she had a bit of an inferiority complex. She may well have developed it in childhood when her parents left her behind, in which case it is unreasonable to blame Alvan for causing it . . . but did he do anything to solve it?

Remarkably, Alvan never spoke of his wife's depression as far as anyone can remember . . . except Phil.

"At the time when we were living in Choma (after Macha), he would tell me things he didn't tell the other siblings. He explained to me about my mom's depression, telling me his side of the story," Phil said. "I remember a time in the garden in Choma when my dad talked to me about my mom. My recollection is that he felt bad that she was depressed and it was a very difficult thing for him and he didn't know how to handle it. It put me in a very uncomfortable position. I remember thinking I was never going to do that as a parent. I think Dad was trying to help me understand both sides, but I felt like I was supposed to choose sides."

Barb surmises that perhaps her mom had a hard time balancing the role of a submissive woman, especially a missionary, with the vivacious and aspiring woman she was. "We always moved for my father's job; we wouldn't have moved for hers," she said. "Perhaps she didn't have a lot of friends and was thought of as quiet at Macha because she didn't learn to speak Tonga very well. We always had people eating with us – nurses, 1-Ws, visitors – I think it's hard to live as a missionary where everyone knows everyone else's business."

Like a good BIC wife, Ardys didn't feel free to express her anger or resentment at things so she internalized her feelings, Barb guessed. As a child, Phil remembers hearing his mother say, "I just wish I would be dead!"

While he heard some people say that Alvan didn't treat Ardys equally or value her opinion, Keith Ulery spoke in Alvan's defense. "You had to be a strong personality to even get to the mission field. There were some ruffled feathers sometimes that you didn't talk about, but we were all strong personalities. When you put six chiefs together, there are no Indians left, but that's what it takes to work on the mission field," he said.

Dorothy Gish, in a separate interview, spoke the same phrase, "To be a missionary you have to be a strong personality. It's just by the grace of God that you don't kill each other."

All who knew the couple agree that they shared the call to missions. Ardys struggled to overcome her depression rather than let it rule her. Sometimes it got the best of her and she retreated to her bed, but who knows how much personal strength and courage she mustered on other days to push through it and not let it drive her down?

"I think she felt right about following Alvan and what he was called to do," Mim Stern said. "I think she liked being a doctor's wife, but the things she couldn't control controlled her, like her depression."

Yet, Ardys could go through periods of life with little crying and no sadness – that's the puzzle of clinical depression.

"There was a strength to Mom that you had to sort of look past this 'weakness,' but I wouldn't even call it that . . . She got a master's and she would've gotten a PhD. if she hadn't been told she was too old. She was victorious, really," Elaine said.

All her life, Ardys continued to be dogged by this thorn in her side, this dark veil of depression that fell like a curtain over an otherwise vivacious woman.

Yet Ardys loved to help and to nurture and, among the Zambians in Macha, it's her reputation as a welcoming hostess and nurturing caregiver that remain.

Selina Moono sits in the dirt outside her thatched roof home, mounds of material scraps at her feet. These she will fashion into rugs and sell in hopes of making some much-needed money.

"Dr. Thuma is so good to the people. He was the one who took care of the widows and poor families. Most of the time, he would come and look after my family because my father died," she said. "Mrs. Thuma would ask, 'What do you need? School fees? Food?'"

Some of her siblings were educated by Dr. Thuma, meaning he paid their school fees. Selina went to school at Macha Mission; her brothers went to Sikalongo. Selina was 12 or so when her father died. He had gone to Zimbabwe for work when he got ill and died. She recalls that Dr. and Mrs. Thuma would come almost every week, bringing food and household needs to the nine children and their widowed mother.

Because her village is close to Macha, the Thumas knew of their need, she said.

She doesn't know how old she is; no one ever told her. But she knows that a white man named Thuma – and his wife – made a huge difference in her childhood and in her faith.

"I remember when he would preach . . . . he would tell the men not to have two wives. And he told her, 'Whatever type of problem you face, do not worry because God is in charge,'" she said.

She looks off across the brown and cracked earth, past her grandchildren who laugh near the family's hut, past the dogs that roam freely in search of a stray peanut and quietly says that she remembers when Dr. Thuma left for the last time. "He said, 'I am leaving you, but as I go, I wish you the best. May you please stay well. I would like to see you again,'" she said and paused before looking heavenward. "We will see each other again."

----- 🌍 -----

Notuya a-Leza
muluyando lwakwe,
Usalazye inzila yesu;
Notwamuswiilila
ukala aswebo,
Abasyoma abaswiilila.

When we walk with the Lord
in the light of his word,
what a glory he sheds on our way!
While we do his good will,
he abides with us still,
and with all who will trust and obey.

Six
Trust and Obey

Daniel Muchimba felt weary and uncertain. Every bone in his body seemed to be rebelling, throbbing with pain and exhaustion. His mind was in no better shape. Was this fight hopeless? How could they overcome and break free? Some days it seemed an insurmountable task, and yet, still Daniel felt a strange mix of exhilaration and expectancy along with all the doubts and reservations that his mind served up regularly. He dragged himself across the Thuma's expansive front yard and up to the door of the strangely-shaped residence. He knocked.

"Daniel, come in!" The door was opened almost instantly by Ardys, who welcomed him with a large smile. "Just in time for tea!"

It was, in fact, well past tea time – both Daniel and Mrs. Thuma knew it – but no matter, hospitality was extended; that was Mrs. Thuma's way.

"Twalumba," Daniel said in thanks and stepped easily into the front parlor. Although this was not an unusual welcome in the Thuma home, it was most unusual in any other white man's home, a fact that was not lost on Daniel. He was used to being left standing out on the stoop at any other white person's house while the occupants talked to him from behind a screen door.

"You always are my friend and I do not forget it," he told Mrs. Thuma as he took a chair. She smiled at him again. "Is Dr. Thuma here?"

"Why, no, he's at the hospital of course; you could find him there," Ardys offered. "But first, tell me how things are going."

Ever interested in the politics of the day, Ardys settled in with cup in hand to listen to Daniel's report about how the freedom fighting was going. Daniel, regional secretary for the United National Independence Party, had plenty of firsthand experiences to share and he sensed that Mrs. Thuma was a sympathetic audience.

"There is fighting in the villages; it is bad," he said. "I do not know if we will succeed," Daniel confessed and poured out all the doubts that had pent up inside him. Mrs. Thuma listened, asking a question here and there or groaning in disbelief.

"We fight among each other; how can we fight united against anyone else?" he said, referring to the conflict among the two African parties fighting amongst themselves even as they fought against the Colonial powers.

Daniel looked down at his lap.

"Daniel, look at me. Look at me," Ardys said and slowly the young man lifted his eyes and met hers. "Daniel, if the Lord be with you, who can be against you?" she stated rather than asked.

It was a watershed moment in the young believer's life. Of course! God alone would give him the courage to forge ahead.

Before Daniel left, he had an invitation to come back the next evening, with his wife, for supper.

"Thank you; Twalumba! We will come!" Daniel said graciously and bowed his head slightly. When he turned from their yard, his step was a little higher and his heart a little lighter. Just being welcomed to sit at Mrs. Thuma's table and hearing her laugh had brightened Daniel's day.

He looked forward to the next evening, when he felt Dr. Thuma would have some more good advice on how to relate to the white people they so desperately wanted to convince of their cause.

It is so good, Daniel thought, that God has given me these friends, my first white friends.

Daniel Muchimba's eyes mist with tears when he recounts those dinners at the Thuma house. He's 88 now, but recollects them as a turning point in his life. Someone believed in him, believed in his cause, and that somehow gave him the strength he needed to keep on fighting.

"I was in the streets fighting for our independence. Dr. Thuma and his wife were a great help to us, advising us how to go about it and not put ourselves in danger," he said. "Dr. Thuma was a different person altogether. Although he was white, he was on our side."

Many an evening, over a bowl of nshima and monkey nuts, Alvan would advise Daniel on how best to relate to the British, how to plainly and courteously state their hopes for their country without appearing rough or threatening. Daniel found this advice irreplaceable. How else would he ever know how to relate to the white man?

But the Thumas' aid didn't stop at the calm and amiable dining table.

"When there would be trouble – clashes or fighting – out in a village, we would send word to Mrs. Thuma to ring the police and within an hour or so, they would come," Daniel said. The Thumas shared a party telephone line at the time and the phone was located in the Thumas' house. Three short rings and three long rings was the "phone number" for the hospital and Ardys was often the "receptionist."

Once, when Daniel was organizing in a nearby village of Mirimba, two members of the National Congress beat him terribly.

"My father and Dr. Thuma came to know I was beaten and Dr. Thuma himself drove to collect me. That's how he was," Daniel said. "Dr. Thuma came to make a difference. We were on his heart."

Ironically, some of the skirmishes were taking place on the very land given to BIC missionary Jesse Engle a half century earlier by Cecil Rhodes, the man who spearheaded British interests in central Africa.

In 1888, Cecil Rhodes obtained mineral rights from some local chiefs and also in that year, Northern and Southern Rhodesia (now Zambia and Zimbabwe) came under British influence. While Southern Rhodesia was granted self-government in 1923, Northern Rhodesia was brought under

British rule. As the years went by, the Africans wanted greater participation in their government. In the early 1950s, the British agreed to have Northern Rhodesia joined in a federation with Nyasaland (now Malawi) and Southern Rhodesia. Under the United Federal party and white settler rule, Southern Rhodesia had gone bankrupt and probably saw alignment with Northern Rhodesia, and its copper wealth, as a ticket back to financial stability. Northern Rhodesia wasn't keen on the affiliation, but that didn't matter. Over the next 10 years, as they had feared, hundreds of millions of pounds were siphoned off to rebuild Southern Rhodesia's economy while Northern Rhodesia's infrastructure – from its roads to its schools and healthcare – fell into disrepair.

Daniel found himself smack in the middle of Northern Rhodesia's struggle for full independence. In 1960, the British government finally acknowledged that the days of colonial rule were ending. A two-stage election in 1962 resulted in an African majority in the legislative council and an uneasy coalition between the two African nationalist parties – Daniel's United National Independence Party and the more militant African National Congress. The council passed resolutions calling for Northern Rhodesia's secession from the federation and demanding full internal self-government under a new constitution and a new national assembly based on a broader, more democratic franchise. When Zambia trade unions, including now powerful miners, threw their weight behind UNIP, the nationalist momentum became unstoppable and the violent rivalry between the two parties was eventually neutralized in a transitional coalition government.

Even though Alvan came from a pacifist background, he grasped the importance of what the Africans were fighting for and saw it more as a struggle for justice, which perhaps enabled him to put aside his personal beliefs about the methods used to achieve it. Also, there wasn't actual fighting with guns as we picture fighting today; it was more like protests and civil disobedience. In fact, many of the skirmishes that Daniel found himself engaged in were actually not with the British but with the African National Congress. The two African parties seemed often at odds with each other for control of the effort.

However, Daniel stressed, Dr. Thuma always encouraged him to act like a Christian. "Although I was a freedom fighter, Dr. Thuma encouraged me to be a Christian. A Christian man can be a better leader, he said," Daniel recalled.

Although they may not have shown it outwardly, the Thumas did feel cautious with the uncertainties of the time. In a letter home in May 1963, Alvan wrote "With the breaking up of the Federation, the future is quite unpredictable so we live a day at a time."

In another letter that summer, he wrote to his parents describing the political situation at great length and saying how it changed daily. The United National Independence Party wanted a new constitution and a new general election by November, he said. The other party, the African National Congress, was having leadership difficulties with many of the top men resigning, which left its leader Harry Nkumbula in a "shakey position."

"Our area is one of the strong areas for ANC and if the party folds up and the government becomes a one party system, our area is likely to suffer a bit," he wrote. "This all points up to the fact that we should live one day at a time."

After independence came in October 1964, Daniel recalled going to the Thuma house to celebrate. "He was so happy. Yes, we danced together!" Daniel declared with a hearty laugh.

Daniel looks at a picture of Dr. and Mrs. Thuma in their later years and tears come to his eyes. He gazes at the picture and runs his fingers over the images. "They were great, great friends," he says.

Perhaps there were hints of it in Alvan's resolve to wear a necktie before the necktie-less Foreign Mission Board or in Ardys' invitation of a black man to her table in a time when that wasn't done, but whatever the origin of their feelings, the Thumas were definitely sympathetic to "bucking the system" if they felt the system needed to be changed.

Barb, the only Thuma child home at the time of independence – the rest were at boarding school in Bulawayo – remembers that her parents were invited to Lusaka for several days of various celebrations. Barb was left with missionaries Graybill and Ethel Brubaker at Choma Secondary School.

The difference that Zambians saw in the Thumas' interactions with them as opposed to other white missionaries is still noted today around Macha.

"Missionaries were missionaries . . . we didn't ask questions . . . they were white people. But then there was Dr. Thuma. He was approachable. He was a good man; he accommodated people," said Jacob Muchimba, who grew up nearby in Sikalongo and was taught at Macha by Ardys.

Lazarus Moono Moonga, a 90-year-old man living in nearby Hamupi Village concurred, "I know there is a difference in our race, but the way Dr. Thuma used to treat us, it showed we are really just one people."

Norma Steckley noted that Alvan's touch toward his African patients was always gentle and they noticed. "He was wonderful. He treated the Africans like a relative," said the 89-year-old retired nurse who now lives at Messiah Village.

Perhaps it was this foundation, this almost-family feeling, which led Alvan to sympathize with the nationals who were trying to gain independence from the British.

"He was a man for all seasons. The Africans could depend on him. He was so respected by everyone for everything," Mim Stern said. "One time, a father came into the hospital with a spear to protect his daughter, who was one of the dressers. (locally-trained women who helped in the hospital as nurse's aides.) A guy was trying to take her away, saying she was his girlfriend. Dr. Thuma called the police and they came. They saved her and later she became the wife of a very respected church man. It was just like Alvan to jump in when he thought there was injustice; to make a difference."

Phil's wife, Elaine, relates that once when Elijah Mudenda, former minister of agriculture and later prime minister of Zambia, stopped by to visit years after the elder Thumas had left Macha, he said that Ardys was the first white person who shook his hand and welcomed him into her home.

"Any of us might have had a black person in our home, but do you see them as someone inferior or as a person of intelligence from whom you could learn something? Alvan's attitude was, 'I'm in their country; I'm going to learn from them,'" observed Dorothy Gish.

Although their support of the struggle for independence was, at the time, noted with disdain by some fellow whites, the Thumas didn't seem to care.

"Other missionaries thought they were becoming too political, getting too close to the African people. They were way ahead of their time and misunderstood by other missionaries," Phil said.

"The word in BIC Missions was that the Sterns and the Thumas were 30 years ahead of their time," Mim recalled. "In those days, you could serve the Africans tea but not a meal. All the mission stations were into that sort of apartheid system. We would just sort of laugh about it."

Missionary Kathy Steubing, who would learn to know the Thumas a half dozen years later, remembers discussing one of those teas with Ardys.

"During the build up to independence, a group of freedom fighters came to Macha and Ardys served them tea and even let them use her indoor bathroom that the family used. Apparently this was not customary," she said. "Ardys being so ready to offer the use of her family's personal toilet, and even offering a clean hand towel, was a clear signal to the visitors that Thumas were not racist and were supportive of Zambian independence. Ardys understood the warm thanks from a Macha native on the delegation as communicating that he was proud of 'our missionaries' who showed such acceptance of the visitors. I think the Thumas were making a political statement about what they thought was Biblical."

Rich Steubing said the couples' similar outlook on racial equality was a building block to their friendship. "I think that's why we got along so well. We came out of the Civil Rights era of the 1960s and we were of the same mind on how wonderful black rule was. I think we were refreshing to each other in our like-mindedness."

Rich thinks the Thumas were ahead of their time in terms of looking at the needs of the country; of seeing that the nationals needed to learn how to do things, not that the missionaries were the saviors who would come in and run things.

"Ardys was fulfilled by the fact that they were able to be a Christian presence and show people that missionaries are forward thinking and supportive of a new regime," he said.

Barb Thuma finds her father's respect for people of other races and religions remarkable considering he came from a conservative BIC background in Ohio. "They tried to be accepting and inclusive. I remember Zambian people eating at our house and people from the Congo staying overnight at our house," she said.

In 1964, the Thumas' term was up at Macha Mission Hospital and the winds of change seemed to be blowing them away from the pioneer work begun at Macha toward new soil that needed some tending.

"There was a known need for expatriate professionals in this new country so my parents believed this was the next thing to do. And yes, I suspect the majority of the other missionaries didn't think like that," daughter Wanda said.

Dr. Bob Worman had come to Macha to work and so it seemed that, with the hospital in good hands, Alvan felt able to move on and support the fledgling government that needed doctors. Shortly after independence, he agreed to go to Livingstone as a general medical officer.

Leaving Macha had to have been bittersweet for Alvan and Ardys, however, their children don't remember much emotion shown externally anyway.

"I do not really remember any farewell parties. My parents were staying in Zambia, just moving away from Macha. Obviously people knew we were leaving," Barb, who was age 7 at the time, said. "As I reflect back, the rationale that I heard from my dad as to why he joined government service was that the Zambian government had asked for and needed medical doctors; and that he would be able to make more money working for the Zambian government and thus would be able to afford to send Meryl and then Phil to college in the USA."

Phil, 13 at the time, remembers just hearing the pronouncement that "The next time you come from school, we'll be somewhere else."

As news of their departure made its way around Macha, Ardys received one of the most significant affirmations of her life; that sounds dramatic, but is likely entirely true. As a sign of admiration, Chief Macha sent her a ceremonial hoe which would have been carried by the chief's wife. The accompanying envelope, marked September 14, 1964, said "On Her Majesty's Service" and was addressed to "Mrs. Doctor Thuma." The letter inside said, in effect, that Ardys was receiving the hoe because, like a chief's wife, "you are royalty."

Ardys displayed that hoe in every home she had after that, perhaps at last tangible proof to her that she was recognized as significant in her role as doctor's wife and as someone who had given much in support of her "chief." When Ardys died, her children decided to offer the hoe back to Chief Macha's family and as far as they know, it resides today in the home of Chief Macha's great granddaughter.

Perhaps the most unusual going-away gift came from a rich and well-known traditional healer near Macha who, when he himself got sick, would come to see Dr. Thuma.

"On the very day that my parents were packed up to leave Macha, this traditional doctor came with a baboon as a gift. Of course it would've been rude to turn it down," said Phil, who was away at boarding school. When he returned home, Jane became his responsibility and good friend.

Cousin Ron Herr, who served as a 1-W in Africa from 1964 through 1966, remembers Jane the baboon. "During the rains, the baboon would take a piece of cloth and move it across her shoulders and over her head and hunker down in the rain, he recalls. "I couldn't believe how human she was."

Thuma children with pet leopard

Having a wild animal for a pet was not unusual for the Thumas. Early on at Macha they had a baby leopard as a pet for about six months and a monkey also joined the family for a time.

Barb remembers the day in November 1964 that her family drove away from Macha in the used VW Kombi that her dad had purchased from the BIC Missions. "It had all our stuff in it plus a steel drum with Jane the baboon. I think there were some missionaries there to see us off and we drove away with all the worldly possessions we had and arrived at Livingstone later that afternoon," she said. "As I think about leaving Macha—I do not think I was sad—as I knew I would visit there again. We were just moving to Livingstone for my Dad's job. Certainly my Dad seemed to be someone who made decisions and moved on – looked forward and not backwards with regrets for what might have been."

Supper that first night in Livingstone marked a definite change in lifestyle for the Thuma family – there were only three at the table for the first time in young Barbara's memory.

"I remember eating a simple supper at a make-shift table – Mom, Dad and me eating soup that Mom had made and we were eating it out of Tupperware bowls and I asked why we were using Tupperware for soup bowls and my mom told me that these Tupperware bowls belonged to her, and all the other plates and dishes that were at Macha did not belong to us, so they were not ours to bring along," Barb said.

The winds of change were also blowing in the public school in Livingstone where Barb went to second grade. "I was there in time to be in the Christmas Musical Program (given) for parents and I remember we all had to learn the new national anthem, as opposed to singing God Save the Queen, for this event," she said.

In Livingstone, the Thumas settled into a nice house provided by the government that had a front veranda, perfect for enjoying lunch together. The Thumas became close friends with Lamar and Anna Mae Fretz, BIC missionaries from Canada who worked at David Livingstone Teacher Training College. They had two children just younger than Barb and the three became fast friends. Barb remembers treks back and forth to each other's houses for meals and playtimes while the adults played cards. Often on Sundays, the two families would picnic along the banks of the Zambezi River.

Thuma residence in Livingstone 1964 – 1965

Money was tight in Livingstone. Although the furnished house was provided, Ardys found herself without much household help – and no cook – for the first time. She picked up the task of daily cooking while Meryl, when home from boarding school, instituted a dishwashing system.

"One person washed dishes; one person dried; one person put the dishes away; and one person got to goof off! I have great memories of this, especially when you got to goof off!" Barb said. "This only worked when there were four of us kids at home, the rest of the time there was no goof-off person!"

Years later, Barb learned from her mom that money was tight at first due to a miscommunication between her dad and the government as to when his salary would commence. Apparently Alvan went for a while without being paid and he had to borrow some money from Meryl and Phil from their "post office savings accounts," which he did pay back. But what a way to start working for the government!

Although her parents were the first people to leave BIC Missions and stay in the country and work for the government, Barb said she didn't sense that they were shunned for their decision. "I always felt that the other BIC missionaries still associated with us and were friendly and certainly when we lived in Lusaka, our home was the 'hotel' for many visiting BIC missionaries, and Mennonite Central Committee Teachers Abroad Program people as well," she said.

Ardys recounted the family's move in "My Story, My Song": "We applied to the Zambian government, which was very short of doctors because of independence (most British doctors had left the country or were terminating in the near future), and they gladly accepted us. We spent several months in Livingstone, where Al filled in for the medical director of the government hospital, who was in South Africa on holiday . . . Later we were sent to Mazabuka, Zambia, where Al was the doctor in charge." (Upon leaving Livingstone, they parted ways with Jane the baboon, which they left behind, much to Phil's disappointment.)

When that short assignment was over, the Thumas were spending one of their last – or so they thought – weekends in Africa attending regional conference at Sikalongo Mission. The family was set to go home on furlough and likely not returning to Africa. Alvan mentioned the impending change in a letter to his sister Elizabeth and mother on April 26, 1965: "Over the weekend, we will be at the Sikalongo Mission . . . This will be our good-bye to most of the mission people here in Zambia." No mention of any feelings about that; just his "As usual, Alvan" closing out the letter.

However, we know from Ardys' writings that, during the foot washing and communion services, Alvan had an encounter with God that would change the course of the family's life again. "Alvan was washing one of the elder Zambian's feet when he thought, 'This will be the last time I have this privilege.' A 'quiet voice' told him it did not have to be; he could again work for the government while still supporting Meryl, who was about to start college in the United States," Ardys wrote in "My Story, My Song."

"Al put before the government the possibility of his serving at Choma if he could return to Zambia . . . For Al to choose his place of service under the Zambian government was a first in all civil service history. You never choose, you <u>went</u> wherever they sent you. But this was our fleece: Choma and return or stay in the United States! Return we did and spent another two and a half years serving God in the Choma area."

During that time, as a government official, Alvan had responsibility for all the mission hospitals and clinics in the district, which included Macha Hospital. Ardys indicated that he looked at the Choma years as some of the best years of his life. "He now could spend time in doing medicine, not building, repairing, etc. etc. etc.," she wrote.

A look into one of the weekly letters home during those years shows the varied work he faced in just one week – this was the week of February 26, 1967. On Tuesday, he was off to Kalomo to testify in the inquest into the death of a man who had died from a ruptured bowel. The man's wife was being prosecuted for the death, but the judge ruled that it was not her fault. Alvan found the day a waste of time since the judge ruled before he ever got to testify, but he did draw some satisfaction from reading through a British Medical Journal and stopping to visit the Kalomo clinic and transporting a number of "cases" – sick patients – home in his Kombi – which was the size of a stretched-out VW Bug.

Thuma home in Choma

"Transporting patients was nothing new for Dad. Every time we went to Choma, we'd put in some TB patients who needed x-rays at Choma Hospital. I remember one time Dad was taking a pregnant woman to Choma because he thought she needed a C-section and then I guess the bumpy road to Choma brought on her delivery and I remember we stopped and Daddy delivered the baby and I watched," Phil said with a shrug. "That was just normal life for us." Wanda has a similar recollection of a different delivery on the way to Choma.

At Choma, Alvan also cared for his first patient with a case of human rabies. A boy about age 12 from nearby Masuku Mission, was bitten by a mad stray dog. His father had refused him to have the series of 14 anti-rabies injections.

Convulsions, vomiting, extreme pain continued and even morphine didn't touch it. A horrendous death. Alvan did a postmortem and sent midbrain sections to the research lab at Mazabuka, which came back positive for Negri bodies – proof of rabies.

Ever eager to document the varied and fascinating medical cases he encountered, Alvan would often ask someone to take pictures of the surgeries or procedures he was performing.

Glenn Schwartz, his former 1-W helper and then a missionary in Choma who is now age 76, remembers when Alvan showed up at his door at 2:30 a.m. and said he had an ectopic delivery to perform and would Glenn come take pictures? "I did. Years later, he showed me the pictures he had kept," Glenn said.

Alvan thought the event so important that he detailed it in a letter to his mother and sister, Elizabeth: "It was one of those rare cases where the vagina had become closed after the woman got pregnant and the baby was presenting itself under the skin near the rectum. I had a case like this several years ago at Macha, but this was a much bigger baby that weighed one pound and five ounces. When I saw what was going to happen, I quickly called Graybill Brubaker to come take pictures of the procedure, but he was away so I ended up getting Glenn Schwartz as the photographer. He was most delighted to serve and I hope he got some good pictures . . . without the pictures to prove it, no one will believe my story. The woman is recovering nicely and I soon must get some pictures of the healed scar."

Alvan, true to doctor form, obviously didn't mince words when sharing graphic details or using anatomically correct language in letters, even to his aged mother! Even in describing the housetraining exploits of their puppy Spot, Alvan wrote that the pup "occasionally uses a rug in the house to relieve bladder pressure."

Ardys was busy teaching at Choma Secondary School, where she taught English and girls' physical education. She loved the work but was very busy. In "My Story, My Song," she calls those years some of the most rewarding of her life.

Mukuwa Kalambo, who would later become executive director of Macha Mission Hospital and then managing director of Macha Research Trust, had Ardys as a teacher in Choma Secondary School for grade 11, English.

He remembers that she was not a boring teacher. "She got us involved in activities rather than just lecturing to us," he said. "She taught us grammar, writing, everything about language," he said.

Ardys was also a coach while teaching at Choma Secondary School; coaching the girls' netball team and girls' track and field team. They won some provincial meets, Barb recalls.

Family life also kept Ardys busy. Her letters are filled with descriptions of the everyday house chores, including cleaning and polishing floors. One night, she noted, that she and Phil shampooed the bedroom rugs while "Wanda and Barb sat on our beds and gave us advice." Ardys dyed some bedspreads and curtains but they didn't come out the color she hoped for so she needed to try again.

Glenn Schwartz is mentioned by Ardys in a letter home; she was planning to have him and his wife for dinner. "Glenn is needing a haircut and he usually comes to Alvan to get it done." Add to Alvan's list of talents one more: Barbering!

The years at Choma kept Alvan's time filled with medical work, but he always had an eye toward the future. He never tired of making plans to better the place where he served and he looked for any opportunity to share those plans with those who might bring them to fruition. Many times, that meant rubbing shoulders with dignitaries and state officials, which took him out of his comfort zone. He did it, however, because it was a necessary means to his end goal.

In November 1966, he wrote to his in-laws about a meeting with the Minister of Health, Executive Officer in the head office and the Deputy Director in the Ministry, who were to be present at the opening of the new leper block at Gwembe Hospital. Alvan had been asked to speak at the ceremony.

"I had imagined him (the Deputy Director in the Ministry) to be a large, forceful person. When he walked in, he had a knit tee-shirt on while the rest had on ties and he was barely five foot tall," Alvan wrote. Then he related to his in-laws the message he attempted to get across to the official: "I tried to get across the idea that Choma is the natural center of the Southern Province and that he should come to see us soon so that plans could be started for the needed expansion in the near future. I told them that Choma Township Council was planning for a larger water supply and that next year would start laying out a new suburb as the population was moving to town and that already 600 houses were being asked for above the present number in the high density housing area." He also included stats on the number of death certificates he had signed, the number of doctors at the hospital and the number of police, all to support his cause before the officials.

One time where he didn't seem to mind – and even was excited by – his proximity to the high and mighty was a day in July 1966 when he served as personal medical officer to the President of Zambia for a day. He wrote about the experience to his mother and sister Elizabeth:

"I was ordered to be there with emergency medical equipment in case there was an accident in landing or take off in this remote area (which was 38 miles up the Zambezi River from the nearest populated area) . . . We had been lined up to be introduced to him and I was highly honored to be No. 4 in the line with the Resident Secretary as No. 1, the Provincial Education Officer next and the District Secretary of Choma just ahead of me." Alvan called the day "possibly the highest honor afforded to me during this tour of service."

Independence was still on Alvan's mind and important enough that he wrote about it in a letter home to Ardys' parents in October 1966. "The 24th is the second anniversary of Zambian independence. This evening, the District Secretary is having a sundowner (cocktail) party which starts at 6:30. We will go to shake hands with the host and hostess and I will drink one orange Fanta and will leave so as to go the church service." (Orange Fantas were Alvan's drink of choice because it could not be mistaken for an alcoholic drink.)

While at Choma, the Thumas celebrated another important anniversary – their 20th wedding anniversary. "The celebration was nothing big, not even a cake, but a little time of remembrance by all of us present," Alvan wrote in a letter to his mother.

It seems hard to fathom that in the midst of such busy lives – full with medical work, travel, housework, childrearing, teaching and countless visitors – that Alvan and Ardys had very much time to devote solely to each other.

While this fact may not have bothered Alvan, one can only wonder how much it affected Ardys. Her depression seemed to worsen after leaving Macha, according to son Phil. She was hospitalized once while in Choma because of it, and it was in Choma that Alvan broached the subject of her depression with Phil in that uncomfortable conversation that he still remembers well. Phil recalled that this marked the second time that his mother was hospitalized for depression; she had been in the Choma Hospital prior to 1966, probably while they were living at Macha.

"In 1966 while I was in boarding school in Lusaka my understanding from my Dad was that Mom did have 'suicidal ideation' as we call it in medical terms, meaning she verbalized the idea that she may kill herself. I do not know that she ever made such an attempt. But I think that it shook up Dad so much that he took her to Lusaka to see a psychiatrist. Barb remembers that she and Wanda stayed with missionaries in Choma for at least several days that time," Phil said. "I remember being taken by my Dad to visit her at Lusaka Hospital and being under the impression that she was receiving electro-shock therapy to try to help her overcome the depression."

Looking back on that time, daughter Wanda wonders if her mother was "burning the candle at both ends" on top of her tendency to depression. "From what we know now about sleep deprivation and how it can make us almost psychotic, I wouldn't be surprised that her workload and maybe self-imposed duties/expectations left her open to the 'breakdown.' She was teaching English full time at Choma Secondary, coaching the netball team in the afternoons, then home to make supper for us, then up late at night correcting all those essays. There would be piles of blue notebooks in the bar area in the front room of the Choma house; she could put them back there and keep them out of sight. Then weekends would be busy with games on Saturdays, up early and then home late on the back of the truck. I know we had someone to help in the house with cleaning and ironing, but she did the bulk of the household stuff. I doubt as an adolescent girl I was much help either!" Wanda said.

Ardys provides a glimpse into her emotional psyche when she writes about the end of their time in Choma. "Again we were at a crisis. By now Phil had returned to the United States for college at Messiah College. I remember that when we went to Lusaka to put him on the airplane, I thought to myself: we left Meryl in the U.S. at 17 years of age, now we are saying good-bye to Phil at 16 years of age. There walks the second son out of my life and it will never be the same; they will be adults when I see them again. There will be no sharing of those fun-loving college days! This is the price I pay as a missionary mother!"

Alvan needed to go to Lusaka on business and so decided to go to the government offices to discuss the termination of his assignment in Choma. He was supposed to finalize their tentative reservations out of Lusaka but by day's end, he had cancelled them and accepted the job as medical director of Lusaka Central Hospital, which was, after the minister of health, considered the foremost medical position in the country. They were to move in a week.

After accepting the Lusaka position, the Thumas were due a leave or holiday and came back to the Grantham area in the summer of 1968. While there, they stayed in several different places, one being an apartment on Grantham Road where former missionaries Lewis and Gladys Sider lived. Wanda relates this interesting story with a twist of espionage involved: "One morning, my father answered a knock at the door and went outside to talk to someone. My mother asked who it was when he came back in. It was a CIA rep who had asked my father to 'help' them and maybe give them information from his new position. He refused to do that, probably because of the Anabaptist separation of church and state as a theological position to some degree. And probably because it would have really impinged on his honesty and trust in that position of power. He was respected in that position because he could mediate apolitically in political/international health incidents," she said, then laughed, "So, a CIA connection in Grantham!"

Next began a three-and-a-half-year adventure in Lusaka, where Alvan saw the Medical School at the University of Zambia come into being. Alvan worked closely with Lusaka Central, which became known as University Teaching Hospital. The complex grew greatly in buildings, staff and patient load under Alvan's direction.

Those three and a half years were demanding of Alvan both medically and socially. He was busy growing the hospital, recruiting teaching faculty and seeing patients. He was primarily an administrator and spent much of his time in the office and at meetings and with architects, since that was a time of rapid expansion of the hospital. While not laying the bricks and mortar himself, Alvan helped make many of the decisions as to how to lay out all the new buildings.

His letters home to his boys during those years recount a busy schedule, full of unusual medical cases, constant administrative decisions about hospital staff and procedure and planning meetings so numerous that Alvan became convinced he couldn't sit a minute longer. "Dad often got tired of all the meetings, etc., so would go to the outpatient clinic in the late afternoon and help the junior doctors working there seeing patients," Phil said. "I met some of these docs in later years and they always commented on how they were amazed that such a senior person was willing to come and work 'in the trenches,' as we would say. But he loved clinical care, and I am sure it was a break from all the administrative headaches."

John Spurrier recalls visiting the University Teaching Hospital with Alvan more than a half dozen years later and watching Alvan stop to greet many people – the cleaners, the cook, the general workers – who all greeted him very warmly. "Finally the current superintendent of the hospital asked Alvan, 'How do you know all these people?' Alvan turned to him and said, 'They worked for me and they work for you; don't *you* know them?'" The relationships he shared with the commonplace staff demonstrated Alvan's attitude that, while his title might be greater, his position was no more important than anyone else.

In his years at Lusaka, as usual, Alvan would not ask anyone else to do what he would not do himself. When his whole staff wanted to go to the First Zambian Medical Congress in Kitwe – all expenses paid by the government – he allowed half the doctors to go and stayed home himself, taking over the Isolation Ward along with his regular duties. To his sister, he wrote, "It sounds as if I didn't do so well in Isolation when I tell you that I averaged four death certificates a day in the ward. I kept Isolation until Tuesday morning. To keep the outpatient department open, I was on duty there from Saturday morning to Tuesday morning, in the fee-paying section and Saturday night, I covered the surgical side of the non-fee paying side. I worked all day Sunday and that is why you did not get a letter from me last week."

Perhaps remembering his little boys' fascination with bugs and the like, Alvan took part of one letter to his boys to recount the story of feeling something moving in his trouser leg during church; something he could not shake out. Then, just as he stood for the last hymn, he felt it again and grabbed hold of his trouser and held it until he was standing. "Out dropped a four-inch gecko, you know those nocturnal lizards with the big eyes and big wide toes. It ran under the bench for a moment and then out past my foot, over the carpet and up the wall a bit . . . I think that he had been in my trousers when I put them on before going to church. I had seen a big one about six inches long in our bedroom when we first moved here and I suspect this to be the mate. We will keep on the lookout for little ones now."

127

Ardys taught at the International School of Lusaka and had the President's twins in her class. She also was a frequent visitor to the hospital, taking along bouquets from her garden to those she visited.

The Thuma house also became an unofficial BIC Hotel of sorts in Lusaka for guests; the proof of which came in the 20 or more sheets in the laundry each week. "Most nights a huge truck would be parked in our driveway, loaded and ready to leave the next day for Sikalongo, Macha or Nahumba Missions. I like to think our home was an oasis in a missionary's busy schedule," Ardys wrote.

For Rich and Kathy Steubing, it was just that.

They stayed at the Thuma home upon landing in Lusaka in January 1970. Rich had come to teach at the David Kaunda Secondary Technical School and Kathy was volunteering there to teach religious education. The Steubings would remain in Lusaka for 12 years. Bishop Frank Kipe had made arrangements for the Steubings to stay with the Thumas for nine nights. They had shipped their crate ahead to their address.

Kathy knew the Thumas by reputation from growing up in Mechanicsburg, Pa. In fact, she remembered their farewell party at the Messiah Home when they were leaving for Africa; Kathy was about 10 at the time.

Now here she was, a missionary's wife herself, being welcomed to her new foreign home by Ardys, whom she called "her orientation" to all things African.

"She took me shopping, taught me the names for things - like naartjie meant tangerine – and she told me where you might not want to walk by yourself at night. She introduced me to the musical society of Lusaka, showed me where she got her hair cut. They just adopted us that first year. I think they saw their missionary role there as mentoring others," Kathy said. "We were young and foolish and now we're old and foolish, but we would've been more foolish without them!"

"We probably saw them at their best; at the pinnacle of their careers," Rich said. "We were very privileged to have been with them at that time."

Thuma home in Lusaka near University Teaching Hospital

Rich remembers Alvan's wry sense of humor and dry wit, an almost British reserve of humor. "One New Year's Eve, a reporter called and asked if there was news and Alvan said 'Oh yes, we've had some cases of poisoning.' The reporter lit up like a Christmas tree. 'Did you find the source?' the reporter asked. 'Yes, we have,' Alvan said. 'Well can you tell us what it is?' Alvan really had the reporter going now! Then he delivered the punch line 'It was 'Chibuku,' which was the local brew of alcohol. He was basically saying people were getting drunk. 'I think you should put that in your paper!' he told the reporter, who was not amused, I'm sure," Rich said.

Rich remembers being impressed that Alvan, the chief medical officer in the country, took his turn seeing patients at the outpatient clinic like any other doctor. "He was the top man in a growing hospital in a big city. He didn't talk a lot about himself, but he was big in those circles," Rich said. He recalls one occasion when Alvan gave the Steubings tickets to see the heads of state arrive for a non-aligned nations summit. Rich and Kathy were thrilled to see Indira Ghandi walk past!

Alvan invited Rich to accompany him to the clinic sometimes and memories are still vivid after all these years.

"Alvan saw that a child was trying to talk with an interpreter about what was going on. He went to the boy and soon he pulled a peanut from this kid's nose with forceps. He had sucked this peanut right up his nose," Rich said. "Next, he showed me an x-ray of a man's knee; the man had jumped into bed and a needle had slipped into his knee and broken off. Al sent him off for surgery. Next, he saw a woman who was aborting a child and bleeding like crazy. I asked him if this was normal for a day in clinic and he said "Maybe not normal, but we do have some interesting cases.' I'll say!"

The Thumas always included the Steubings in what their kids were doing and would invite them to go see their musicals or to go along to the pool.

"Another job that Ardys had was hospitality for people from Choma or Macha who came to Lusaka for supplies. A good bit of her salary went to the costs of hospitality for these guests who would show up unannounced and stay for dinner and a night or two. They saw this as part of their missionary work," Kathy said. "We realized what a gift this was because after they left, people thought we would pick up where they left off and we couldn't afford it. Ardys really ran a bed and breakfast with dinner!"

In 1969, Glenn and Verna Schwartz were living in Livingstone at the Teacher Training College when Verna had a miscarriage. Doctors gave her a shot in her shoulder to contract her uterus. Later, she started having pain in her shoulder and a subsequent x-ray showed a wire was left in a muscle from the injection. The best place to have it removed was Lusaka and so they flew to Lusaka, where Alvan met them and oversaw the surgery. Then, during recuperation, Verna stayed in the Thuma home. She will never forget hearing the radio broadcast of the first American landing on the moon while there. She recalls that Ardys was "very proper" "very precise" and a good hostess.

Ardys, social by nature and no longer surrounded by missionary women to whom she felt inferior, flourished in Lusaka. Here, she was doing what she had been trained for – teaching – and what she loved – hostessing. She also enjoyed rubbing shoulders with the dignitaries and people in high positions whose company Alvan's medical post gained them.

In Lusaka, Ardys seemed to gain respite from her depression. The Steubings, perhaps their closest friends at the time, saw nothing of it.

"We think she really enjoyed the change from primitive Macha to the city life of Lusaka and her teaching job. Because of Alvan's position, they were invited to lots of upper echelon events, parties etc. It was a world away from Macha," Kathy said.

In Lusaka, Ardys had the chance to have many more friends, to sing with the musical society, to get dressed up for social occasions.

"She was a talker. We were cut out of the same mold. When we went places, people would ask us if we were sisters or mother and daughter," Kathy said.

There were times though when the depression reared its head. Barb remembers crying about it once in Lusaka because she didn't understand what was wrong with mom. Her dad's explanation: it was partly due to menopause.

Ardys talked about how much her teaching meant to her in a letter to her mother-in-law and sister-in-law Elizabeth in August 1969: "Did I tell you that I have been asked to teach Grade 4 next school year? The Principal wanted to give me a problem sort of group to see if I could give them a little extra TLC and push getting them ready for the upper school. I thought it was something of a compliment and have accepted the challenge. Mr. Quimby said, 'Mrs. Thuma, I'm warning you it is going to be a very difficult job, but I think you are the one for the job and would like you to try it.'"

Perhaps hinting at her tendency toward depression, Ardys noted that both her daughters urged her to take the challenge because it would "keep me from getting into a rut." But, Ardys countered, "I certainly haven't had a chance of getting in a rut since going back to the classroom!"

As Alvan's contract was coming to an end, he reflected on the transition ahead in another letter to his sister, Elizabeth in April 1970: "The way things look, this will be possibly the last holiday (vacation) we will take in Africa. I'm coming to the end of my contract and I know of no one who would renew a contract like my present job calls for. Our plans are beginning to take shape. Wanda takes her General Certificate of Education "O" level exams in November and this is the equivalent of graduating from high school. I figure this is a good time to make a change." He goes on to write that Wanda would be set to enter Messiah College and Barb, age 13, would be in her first year of high school and able to adjust to life in America.

Then, as if processing what the move will mean personally, he reflects and refers to himself in third person, "The biggest adjustment will have to be made by the parents, I know, after having had our roots in Central Africa for almost 20 years. Possibly it will be so cold in the East that we will turn around and head back for Africa. Maybe we should put out a fleece to the effect that we will have to arrive on a hot day in January if we are to stay."

Even a matter-of-fact person like Alvan surely had to feel some emotion at leaving the African soil upon which he had built his medical career, lived such an extraordinary adventure, but more than that, honored his calling from God.

One can only imagine whether he had the urge to visit Macha Hospital one last time before he left; to run his hands over the bricks that he laid; to touch the soft skin of an African child, representative of so many small lives he had saved; to wander among the patients' families camped out at "the fires" behind the hospital and laugh with them as they offered him monkey nuts or nshima.

Did he wonder to himself if he had indeed accomplished his mission "to share the gospel through medicine" that he laid out in a sermon before he ever left American soil?

"One of the motifs I think I learned from my parents is that as a Christian, you try to follow what seems to be God's will for your life. And if a door opened that seemed to indicate that, you followed," Wanda said.

In January 1971, the door to America – and home to Ohio – swung open wide and beckoned Alvan and Ardys home.

But what if home didn't feel like home anymore? For Alvan and Ardys, home would partly always be the red soil of the African bush that stained their hearts with a love that could never be washed away.

----- ⌇ -----

Nombungano yakwe mukasame nyoonse;
Tulaya bulwana, tulwa a-Saatani.
Musolozi wesu uli Kristo Jesu;
Uli Mwami, Musunguli; uli Mufutuli.

Onward, Christian soldiers, marching as to war,
with the cross of Jesus going on before.
Christ, the royal Master, leads against the foe;
forward into battle see his banners go!

SEVEN
Onward Christian Soldiers

"Oh, don't you look beautiful!" Ardys gushed as she beheld her granddaughter Lynette in the wedding gown she had worn to marry Alvan 50 years earlier.

"Oh yes, so pretty!" Barb exclaimed as she smiled broadly at her young niece in the form-fitting dress with an embroidered overlay and a lovely sweetheart neckline. Lynette twirled in delight as Barb snapped a picture. Wanda, also visiting her parents in their Ohio farmhouse, joined in the memory-making moment, smiling warmly at brother Meryl's middle daughter.

Janae, Lynette's younger sister, watched from across the room, gazing at her taller, more slender sister with a hint of envy. She knew there was no point in her trying the dress; it probably wouldn't fit.

She didn't notice her grandpa had come to the doorway. "Janae, follow me," Alvan whispered in her ear and she almost jumped because she hadn't heard him approach. She got up quickly and slipped out of the room, glad for a chance to retreat.

"Let's go have some fun of our own," Grandpa Thuma said conspiratorially and beckoned Janae to follow him outside.

Once out in the warm summer sun of Darke County, Ohio, Janae brightened. She loved her visits to her grandparents' farm. No schedule, no parents, no schoolwork beckoning.

Alvan led her to his old pick-up truck in the field near the house and opened the driver's side door. "Get in, young lady," he told her. She looked at him with disbelief; they both knew she was too young to drive. "Get on in there! We're going driving!" he repeated.

Janae climbed in the driver's side and Alvan slid into the passenger's seat. "Now start her up and let's go," he said, smiling at her.

Janae grinned. How did Grandpa know that she had watched Lynette drive the truck with Grandpa so many times and envied her each and every time?

"Who cares about an old wedding dress anyway? I'm going on an adventure!" she said to herself with wild abandon as she jerked the old truck forward and her grandpa pretended to just narrowly save himself from going through the windshield.

"We want to live to taste your grandma's supper," Alvan said wryly.

Janae looked over at her grandfather and smiled, "Thanks Grandpa."

Janae Thuma Figueroa, now 36, remembers summers spent on her grandparents' Ohio farm as some of her best moments of childhood. Alvan teaching his grandchildren to drive in the farm pick-up is an oft-mentioned story, but for Janae, it's her sweetest memory of her grandpa exactly because she knows he noticed her dejection that day and came to her rescue.

"To me, Grandpa was always cool and calm, like a giant tree. I always felt attracted to that calmness and strength, but he was often distant," Janae said. "But he had a sweet side that he showed when the time was right."

On her summer forays from her native home of Honduras to the amber waves of grain in Ohio farm country, Janae looked forward to getting to know her father's parents whom she rarely saw. Most of all, she loved being the center of her grandmother's attention. There was no end to the advice given and secrets shared over a batch of cookie dough or a basket of laundry.

"I loved both my grandparents very much, but my heart always pulled me nearer to grandma. I always felt that she needed my attention during the summers my sisters and I spent at the farm," Janae said. "Often, Michelle and Lynette would work outside helping Grandpa doing what was deemed 'fun' jobs and got paid for it. I always stayed inside and helped Grandma with the house chores – dishes, laundry, setting the table, cooking. Because I chose to stay in with Grandma, I feel I had a more intimate relationship with her. She often talked to me and opened up about how she felt about grandpa and my father. I saw her cry many times. To me grandma had this elegance and intelligence, she was very loving and she always made me feel special."

Janae treasures a photograph taken of her on her 10th birthday at her grandparents' farm. Ardys would always make her granddaughter's favorite meal of curried lamb and an angel food cake with funfetti frosting. Lynette also remembers her grandma's famed curried lamb and her African peanut butter dishes.

Back home in Ohio, Alvan and Ardys seemingly settled well into a new routine – Alvan once again a country doctor and Ardys teaching at the local elementary school – but who knew how hard it really was on them to adjust from life in the African bush to America in 1971?

Did Apollo 15's mission to the moon seem as far away as Africa? Did Alvan wonder why all the fuss over the opening of Walt Disney World in Florida that year? Did he watch the debut of "All in the Family" and wonder how anyone could identify with Archie Bunker?

Was it, as Alvan has suggested in his letter to Elizabeth, the hardest adjustment for himself and Ardys?

Wanda guesses her mother may have preferred to relocate to California, where she had her roots, but a vacancy opened up in the Arcanum medical building and "it was only logical" that Alvan would take it. The family settled into a modest home on Woodside Drive in Arcanum, near the office building.

Barb remembers the transition was hard on the entire family. "When I came back in ninth grade, it was difficult because my life to that point had been very different from other kids my age. I wanted to fit in and have what was cool, but I didn't know what was cool," she said.

She thinks her mother struggled more with the loss of their African life than her father. "Daddy had his profession still. She was used to being the wife of a semi-important man, going out to cocktail parties, etc. and now they landed in middle America. She would want to invite people over and he'd say, 'No don't,'" Barb recalled.

Thuma home on Woodside Drive, Arcanum, Ohio

Alvan settled into an established medical practice in Arcanum, in an office building that he shared with several other doctors. Later, he also became part-time medical director of the Church of the Brethren Retirement Home in Greenville, a post that would turn fulltime after his retirement from private practice. He also visited many elderly people in several of the nursing homes in the Greenville area on a monthly basis.

"Dad definitely enjoyed working with the elderly, was very patient and kind, and also spent his time working with insurance claims and committee and paper work for the Brethren home," Phil said.

Dr. Sam Brubaker, fresh out of four years of surgical training, joined the surgical practice of Dr. Leroy Steinbrecher in 1973. Sam's father-in-law Paul Lenhert and Dr. Jesse Heise, as well as Alvan, had offices in the same building.

"It must've been a step down from Zambia, where he was a medically prominent person, to Darke Co. to step into the role of a country doctor, but he did it very graciously," said Sam, who was on staff with Alvan at Wayne Hospital. Both also had in common their membership in the BIC church – the Thumas at Pleasant Hill and the Brubakers at Fairview.

"He was so mild-mannered. He certainly didn't project himself. People never knew he went to formal dinners in Zambia with presidents and prime ministers. You mostly heard about these things from Ardys," Sam said. "Hospital personnel probably heard more about Al Thuma in Africa from Steinbrecher than they did from Thuma."

Jesse Heise, now 92 and living at the Brethren Retirement Home, remembers his colleague as "a good fellow" who was – and he repeated this four times – "kind, gentle, soft spoken."

Jesse recalled a short-term assignment he completed at Macha Hospital from 1968 to 1969 when Alvan was in Lusaka. "Al visited Macha while I was there. I noticed he stooped down and inspected the concrete work at the hospital. I assumed he had been instrumental in putting it there and he was interested to see how it had withstood the test of time and nature," he said.

Alvan was "serious minded with high ideals and goals and very dependable with patients," Jesse recalled. He also noted that the former African doctor didn't talk a lot about himself.

Ardys got a job teaching elementary school at the Arcanum-Butler Local Schools and was beloved by her students and fellow teachers alike until her retirement in 1985.

"Ardys Thuma was a special person in my life and an influence in my teaching career," said Cindy Sink, who began teaching second grade at Arcanum in the fall of 1978. "Mrs. Thuma was already there teaching second grade. Being a new teacher, Mrs. Thuma took me under her wing and helped me along the way; she became my mentor. I remember her as being very kind and a wonderful teacher to the students."

Unlike her husband, Ardys often talked about her mission work in Africa, Cindy recalled.

Millyellen Strayer was one of Ardys' last students in her second grade year of 1984. Africa, Millyellen recalled, was a frequent topic of conversation in their classroom.

"Mrs. Thuma had a distinct voice that you listened to when she told a story," said Millyellen, now 36 and married to Drew Strayer, a pastor at Manor Church in Lancaster, Pa. "She often brought in African artifacts – wooden zebras, giraffes – and told stories about being a missionary in Africa."

Although Ardys was firm and ran an ordered classroom, she was kind and made her young students want to please her, Millyellen said.

"Mrs. Thuma was also very compassionate. If she saw you were upset, she was very quick to put you on her knee and ask you about your problem," she said.

One wonders, was Ardys doing for these young children what she wished someone would have done for her when she was young and upset? Did she still long for someone to reassure her that everything would be OK?

When Millyellen got married in 2000 and had a reception/shower at the Dillsburg (Pa.) BIC Church, Ardys came. She would have been living at Messiah Village in Mechanicsburg, Pa. at that time.

"I don't know how she knew, but she told me she came because she remembered me," Millyellen said. "She was quite frail. It was wonderful to see her. She didn't stay long, but I remember she patted my face . . . It was very sincere."

Always a people person, Ardys sought out and greatly enjoyed community involvement in Arcanum. She was the church organist and pianist, a garden club member and a proud member of the Daughters of the American Revolution and went to great lengths to prove her rightful presence in the club. She still loved to entertain but was, as ever, held back in her exuberance by a husband who was too tired for company at the end of a long day practicing medicine.

Ardys was also very active in her local teachers' association. Ron Herr remembers talking shop often with Ardys. "She was always talking issues. She was president of her local teacher's organization and I was head negotiator for my teacher's organization in Trenton so we had a lot in common. She was always engaging. She seemed to be interested in justice; the rightness or wrongness of policies," he said. He recalls being at a teachers' meeting where the entertainment was square dancing. He didn't know if she would join in or not because it was DANCING! She didn't but she told Ron, "Just enjoy." She wasn't going to try to keep him from dancing even though she would not dance herself.

"I thought they were more modern in their thinking and doing than the typical BIC people I grew up with," Ron said.

With the full support of Alvan, Ardys worked on and earned a master's degree in education from Wright State University in 1974 at the age of 50. While one would think this achievement would have bolstered Ardys' self-esteem considerably, she apparently still judged herself harshly.

Perhaps this constant comparison game left her feeling distant from other women because here, as in Macha, Ardys didn't have any good female friends, according to Barb.

"She had no one to tell things to. I think she did compare herself to other people a lot and she cared about what people thought more than she should have, in my opinion. I don't think she had the best self-esteem but she certainly instilled some good self esteem in us," Barb said.

Lynette remembers her beloved Grandma as an emotional person, but points out that maybe this personality trait stuck out more obviously in the Thuma family where emotions are held close to the vest.

"As a child and young adult, I was not aware of Grandma's depression. I remember my Dad and Grandma getting into arguments which seemed to get quite heated. I do not remember Grandpa stepping in to support Grandma during these times," she said.

In 1981, the Thumas bought a farm in nearby Bradford that had been the homestead of Alvan's mother Fanny and then was owned for many years by his Uncle Jake Etter (his mother's brother), who was an Old Order River Brethren Bishop.

Back on a farm, Alvan seemed to thrive, perhaps remembering all the good times he had growing up on his own family farm. He tended an expansive garden and constructed what was deemed the largest farm pond in Darke County and stocked it with fish. He had 20 or more sheep and loved to help birth the lambs. He also loved to look out the window and see them 'safely grazing' in the field – as in Bach's cantata – Phil said. Alvan also bought and fattened steer to sell, usually no more than five or 10 at once.

Family Homestead near Bradford, Ohio

"Land was important to Uncle Al," said Ron Herr. "When we visited there, Aunt Ardys was talking, talking, talking and Uncle Al would take me out to the barn and show me his garden. He had bees for his pear tree pollination. He also had strawberries; later, he would crawl down the rows to pick them when he didn't have the strength to walk along the row to pick them."

Sam Brubaker also recalls Alvan's tours of his gardens and fish pond. "Alvan enjoyed the country life," his colleague remarked.

It was on this farm that Meryl's children learned to drive in Grandpa's old pickup.

"He taught me how to drive with his gray single cab pick-up truck, manual transmission and no power steering!" Lynette said. "First, I got to practice on his riding lawn mower. Then, after some supervised practice, he would let me practice driving on my own in the pasture. He would set up buckets for me to practice the 'maneuverability test.' He took me for my driver's license test."

Perhaps eager to instill in his granddaughter his own work ethic, Alvan would pay his grandchildren for working around the farm. Lynette recalls all the paying jobs that Grandpa gave her – things like painting the milk house, puttying the barn windows, mowing the lawn, harvesting strawberries and potatoes from his garden and helping to move dead sheep from the barn.

Old bank barn at house near Bradford, Ohio

Lynette, who went on to become a doctor, recalled that Alvan helped her get her first job in the medical field, at the nursing home where he was medical director at the time. Lynette was trained and employed as a certified nursing assistant.

She has wonderful memories of summers spent at her grandparents' farm. Ardys would take her shopping, allow her to tag along to lunch dates with teacher friends and taught her to play the piano one summer.

"She kept a clean and beautiful home. She was always well dressed and a beautifully elegant lady," Lynette said. "She was very social, talkative, proper and polite. I remember during family reunions, I would always make sure I sat at her table because she was the life of the table in a positive way. Then I was very shy and quiet and Grandma would save me from social situations which I found very awkward and uncomfortable."

Lynette remembers that Ardys would travel to visit their family in Honduras, but Alvan would never accompany her. She especially treasured that her grandmother came to her high school graduation.

"Every Christmas when Dad and/or Mom would travel to the U.S., they would come back with a whole suitcase full of individually-wrapped gifts from Grandma. This was always the highlight of Christmas for me; it must have taken her hours and hours to find all those gifts and then individually wrap each one." Her grandma, she noted, remembered every single birthday with a card and accompanying check, even when she was an adult.

The days of summer vacation always fly away fast, but for Lynette, the memories of their adventure have lasted a lifetime. "I remember we would drive around farm fields to collect milkweed and we would also collect butterfly cocoons off of Grandma's pear tree. We would put the cocoons in a jar with milkweed and watch monarch butterflies 'be born' and then we would then let them go," Lynette said. "Lots of memories!"

As the years went by, it seemed to family that Alvan and Ardys grew further apart in their interests and in their affection for one another.

Ardys remained the social butterfly while always-reserved Alvan seemed to withdraw further into his cocoon.

"My impression was that they had grown apart. Mom was very frustrated because Dad wouldn't talk to her about his feelings. She told me that she told Dad they needed to go to marital counseling and he only went once. I wasn't able to say to my dad, 'Why aren't you willing?' In my way of thinking, he gave up on trying to make the relationship better. He'd tried for 20 years," Phil said.

"They didn't argue very much; I think my mother would've preferred to have things out, but my dad clammed up," Barb said.

Perhaps Ardys was finally accepting the fact that Alvan was going to be like the standard closing of every letter he ever wrote: "As usual". . . He was not going to change; he was not going to become an extravert, a dashing host of parties, a consoling shoulder to cry on when she was down.

Phyllis, Ardys' younger sister, remembers that when Ardys came to visit her in Oregon, she remarked that Alvan didn't want to go anywhere. "We tried to brainstorm with her on ways to get him out. I think he got more conservative," Phyllis said.

Money – or rather, attitude toward it – seemed to be a source of friction at times. They had learned to be frugal in the missionary years when money was tight. Ardys had grown up on the west coast, where she enjoyed a cultured life and dressing smartly. Her two younger sisters had married well and no doubt Ardys envied their nice American lifestyles a time or two when she was hoping the water supply would hold out in her crude African kitchen.

Now, back in Ohio and earning an income herself, Ardys did gain permission from her husband to open her own checking account, but found she faced an internal struggle.

"On the one hand, she couldn't spend what she wanted on nice things earlier in her life, and when she got to the point where she could, she found she didn't have the conscience to do it," Wanda said.

Her husband's example of frugality certainly set the bar high.

Meryl recalls a childhood memory of finding a whole cigarette on the ground and picking it up. "My parents taught us you never waste anything. I found this whole cigarette still burning on the ground. I picked it up and said, 'Look, Dad, this is a whole cigarette,' thinking we shouldn't waste it. He told me to put it down and he smashed it and said, 'That has to be one of the dirtiest habits there ever is,' and now, as an old man, I agree," Meryl said.

Dorothy Gish recalls that Alvan had just two suits; one was a khaki wash n' wear that he wore every Sunday and the other was a gray pinstripe that he kept for special occasions. Everyone grew quite tired of seeing the khaki suit, she said. "One day when he had his gray suit on, a bird that had been eating mulberries dumped on his shoulder – the stain was impossible to get out. We all said, 'Why couldn't it have been his wash and wear?'" she said, laughing.

Dr. Daniel Berger, now 61, was a young doctor aspiring to achieve great things when he worked with Alvan at Wayne Hospital in 1982. Perhaps that's why he remembers being struck most by Dr. Thuma's simple lifestyle.

"He had an old AMC car and his antenna was an old coat hanger he had stuck down in the hole where the antenna should be," Daniel said. "Wherever he spent his money, it wasn't on himself."

Her sisters knew that Ardys was becoming increasingly frustrated with her husband. His frugality was no surprise – here was a man who had sold his blood to gain money for college tuition! But perhaps, in this later season of life, Ardys longed to break out of the mold that held them so strongly for so many years while, by contrast, Alvan seemed to cling closer to it.

"Al came from a very conservative area of Ohio. Maybe the older he got, the more he got into those conservative ways. He was more of a recluse later in life," Marylou observed.

In the Ohio years, as in all of their married life, depression was the "other woman" that lurked beneath the surface and damaged their relationship in ways perhaps neither of them even understood.

"I think over many years, my dad not knowing how to handle the depression put him into a shell and he just withdrew," Phil said.

Even as a child, Janae picked up on her grandma's depression, although it was never openly discussed, she said.

"I am not sure if I understood then that she suffered from depression, but now I recognize it because I myself seemed to have inherited that struggle," Janae shared. "The end of the summer was always hardest for Grandma. I am not sure if it was because of the fact that my father was there or because we were leaving, maybe it was both. Often times my father and Grandma would get into verbal arguments – these arguments were instigated by my father and their relationship often seemed strained – and Grandma would just go to her room and stay there until we left, just coming out to say one last goodbye. We were always told that Grandma had a stomach ache, which I think may have had some truth to it as often stomach problems are associated with depression."

Meryl recalls that his mother retired from teaching school at age 62 because she had a persistent flu and Alvan advised that she might as well retire. "She did and got immediately better – and most angry that she had retired. I think it was psychosomatic, stress-induced," Meryl said.

His mother's depression left a deep impression on the Thumas' oldest son, who said he was glad to go away to boarding school because it kept him away from his mother's bouts of depression for nine months of the year. "She would go to bed and say her tummy hurt. My dad never talked about it with me. I think he tried to cover it up. I think he thought it was embarrassing," Meryl said.

After Meryl was grown and married, his mother visited him in Honduras, where he built and founded Progreso International School and now serves as administrator and teacher of the 250 pupils in Kindergarten through 12th grade.

"Just before a bout of depression, she would get very critical. I remember she was here in Honduras visiting me and she got very upset that I became a Baptist minister. There were no BIC churches here; I thought she should be happy that I became a pastor," he said. As an adult who never forgot how his mother's depression affected his life, Meryl said, "I never dreamed of getting married to woman who is depressed. It messes up your life."

Phil too remembers that he would clash with his mother, but also knows it was partly his fault because he admits he was intolerant.

"I was in my second year of medical school in 1971. I picked my parents up at the airport and told them I was engaged. It was rude, in retrospect. And Elaine wasn't even Brethren in Christ!" he said with a chuckle. "I was in that stage of rebellion. At that stage of my life, my mother bugged me and I didn't like to talk to her. We wrote letters, but we didn't call. Elaine had to force me to go visit."

Like his brother, Phil said he found it was "just easier" not to be around his mother because he worried, "What if I say something that throws her into a depression?" Phil said this made him become very independent.

Their relationship did improve, although Phil doesn't know when. "As I got older, I was willing to be tolerant of Mom," he said.

In between her struggles, however, Ardys loved life and lived it to the fullest. She packed a full schedule and even considered pursuing a doctorate degree after completing her master's.

One of her closest friends in Ohio was Sam's wife, the late Lucy Brubaker, who worked as an occupational therapist. "The women were good friends; they had a lot of history in common," with Ardys being good friends of her parents, Sam said.

Surprisingly, Sam knew nothing of Ardys' depression and was surprised to hear about it. "Lucy never remarked that Ardys was depressed or was a hard friend to have. Of course we never lived in a mission setting with them, where stressors would have unmasked some of this stuff," Sam said. "Perhaps one projects one's own perspective on other people, but I never thought Ardys felt she gave up more than she had gained. Neither Lucy nor I ever sensed that she felt negatively toward her life."

As far away as life in Africa must have felt in Arcanum, there came a year in the mid-1970s when the Thumas decided to go back to Macha. It was a year that would prove as much as things change, they stay the same.

----- 🌍 -----

Cita mboyanda, Mwami Mubumbi,
Uli Mubumbi, ndili bulongo;
Mwami, ndibumba, mbuli mboyanda,
Mbwencilindila, Mwami Mubumbi.

Have thine own way, Lord! Have thine own way!
Thou art the potter, I am the clay.
Mold me and make me after thy will,
while I am waiting, yielded and still.

Eight
Have Thine Own Way

There had been many times in the past several months that Dr. John Spurrier wondered what he had gotten himself into by coming to Macha, but perhaps none more than this moment, standing in the operating theatre, nursing students at his side, patient open on the table . . . and clueless what to do next.

Dr. Alvan Thuma, founding physician of Macha Hospital and legendary in the surrounding community, stood next to him. Earlier in the day, when this patient presented with an incarcerated right inguinal hernia, John had confessed he didn't know how to do the surgery. He had done hernia operations before but never one that was stuck out and could not be reduced back into the abdomen. He suggested the man should be referred to Choma Hospital, but Alvan had goaded him into trying, reassuring him that "Oh sure we can!" and he would be there with him in the surgery. Now here they were and Alvan was no help! "You got me into this. Now what?" John asked Alvan.

"I don't know! You're the surgeon!" Alvan replied.

"Oh great! Just great!" John huffed. If he were a swearing man, now would be just the right time, he thought. With much anxiety and even more prayer, John muddled through the operation successfully. Later, Alvan told him, "See, I knew you could do it!" It was all John could do not to retort, "No thanks to you!"

The year ahead was going to be full of surprises and challenges, John knew that much. Yes, he and his wife Esther wanted to serve God through medical missions, but here? When their original idea of going to

151

the Navajo Mission Hospital in New Mexico fell through and the suggestion of Macha Hospital was advanced, John and Esther had both replied, "We don't think so!" But "time and God and who knows what else?" had changed the young couple's minds and they had followed "a reluctant call" to the African bush.

With just a year of surgical training under his belt after medical school, John had moved his wife and 19-month-old daughter across the globe from family and home. While the terrain, the living conditions and the color of the people were all foreign to the Pennsylvania family, at least Alvan Thuma was a welcome and reassuring sight – most of the time.

Wherever they went together, people gushed over Dr. Thuma.

"You saved my life!"

"Without you, my baby would have died!"

"I named my son after you!"

"If we just touched you, we got better!"

All the accolades seemed to make Alvan uncomfortable. He brushed them off with a forced smile or an awkward silence.

But when it came to telling John stories about the building of the hospital and his life in the African bush in the 1950s, all silence was broken. The man could talk for hours and hours about that, John thought to himself with a chuckle.

Just then, John looked across the dirt road to the hospital and saw Alvan with a hoe, digging trenches to water the fruit trees he had planted two decades ago. Next, he was trimming the trees – where did he get all this energy after seeing patients all day, John wondered.

Then it occurred to him – Alvan probably couldn't find enough hours in the day to pack in all the things he wanted to do in the year he was back at Macha. What would it be like, John wondered, to return to an expanding, bustling hospital and know that it stood, that it saved lives, because of you?

Suddenly John felt a yearning well up in his soul and a prayer forming on his lips; "Oh Lord, take my life and use it for your glory. Give me passion! Take these hands of mine and work through them to heal and to save the lives of these wonderful people!"

As John Spurrier reflects back on his first year at Macha Hospital, he realizes what a blessing it was to share it with

Alvan Thuma, despite the older doctor's propensity for getting them into sticky situations.

"It was wonderful for me. It was an introduction to the people by the man who started the hospital," John said. "Of course, there were times in surgery when I wanted to strangle him!
He pushed me beyond my comfort zone and abandoned me! But I learned a lot!"

When Alvan left Macha in 1964, he no doubt hoped he would one day return. That day came in July 1975 when he was able to leave his practice in Arcanum in the reliable hands of his youngest son, now a doctor also, for an entire year.

"While I was in my internship year from July 1974 to June 1975, in Dayton, Ohio, we often drove up on weekends to visit Mom and Dad in Arcanum. One time Dad and Mom said they would like to go back to Zambia for a year in late-1975 to mid-1976, and Dad asked me if I would be willing to cover his practice for a year and earn some money to pay off our school debts. I am not sure this was something he had been planning for a long time - but I think they both had wanted to go back, and this was also his way of helping us financially without giving us money outright," Phil said. "So after my internship ended on June 30, we worked together for a few weeks for him to orient me; then they left for Zambia."

The local newspaper carried news of the arrangement. "The elder Dr. and Mrs. Thuma are pleased to have their son, daughter-in-law and new granddaughter, Jennifer, four and one half months old, with them. 'They will stay in our home while we are in Zambia,' said Mrs. Ardys Thuma, mother of Dr. Philip."

The story went on to describe how Alvan had founded Macha Hospital and how he would return to the outlying clinics in the African bush to see patients. In what now reads as a humorous foreshadowing – considering John Spurrier's comments – Ardys is quoted as saying "The doctor will probably do some surgery also." Ahem!

When Alvan returned to Macha, he found a campus that had grown and changed in the years since his departure.

Behind the original men's and women's wards, there now stood the pediatric ward, the TB ward and the maternity ward. The outbuildings that Alvan had built to house the outpatient department and lab now found other uses as housekeeping and the TB clinic. Additional staff houses dotted the perimeter of the hospital grounds and a nurses' training school was located up the road. The Macha Girls School, built in the late 1960s, was a new addition to Macha as was a dam and large concrete water tower up on the hill. A small open-air chapel behind the main hospital had been added, which Alvan probably figured was preferable to the service location he had used out on the grass beside the hospital when he held Sunday morning chapel for patients and staff.

The Thumas settled into a staff house down the dirt road from the main house that had been theirs. Did it seem odd to them to return to a place so familiar and dear, a place where time stood still in their memory, but certainly a place that had expanded and changed in reality?

"I wondered what Alvan thought when he returned. It's hard to see someone take over what you started and maybe do things differently," said Erma Jean Bert, now 74, who was serving as a nurse with husband, Sam, now 69, who was serving in hospital administration and business management in the year that the Thumas were there. "I wonder whether he thought his vision was carried out or not when he left it to the Zambians."

Whatever his thoughts of the present state of things at Macha Hospital, Alvan apparently didn't share them with anyone. Ever a steady presence, he stepped right back into the daily hospital routine and fell back into the long hours he kept when he was in charge.

Alvan never seemed to get frustrated with the long hours or the repeat patients or the questions someone would stop and ask him even as he was finally walking out the door of the hospital after a long day, John said.

"He would work in the hospital all day and after work, he would go with his hoe and dig trenches and start watering the fruit trees he had planted. Then he would trim them," John said. "He didn't like it if people didn't stick to the designated paths around Macha. I can still hear him yelling, 'Kwiina nzila' from the veranda, which means 'nothing path.'"

Ardys began teaching at the Macha Girls' School and, as neighbors to the Spurriers, she took on a grandmotherly role with their daughter, Becca. In fact, Esther remembers that her young daughter's first sentence was, "Auntie Ardys bringed the cucumbers."

Out and about in the community, Zambians flocked to Alvan, welcoming him back with high compliments, out-of-this-world testimonies of how he had "healed" them or someone they knew and accolades that he accepted with reluctance.

"He had a self-depreciating chuckle. I think there must've been a great sense of satisfaction for him to hear these things, but I don't feel like he displayed arrogance in any way I saw," Esther Spurrier said. "On the other hand, he was the star of many of his stories!"

For Ardys, the year in Macha proved more challenging than she anticipated, or she may not have gone. Then again, she probably would have gone since she was used to a lifetime of putting her needs behind others' needs.

"At Macha, she was living out Alvan's life. It was unquestioned that the wife would follow the husband wherever his interests took him. I think she felt greatly what she was sacrificing, but I never heard her complain," Esther said.

Many surmised that it might have been hard on Ardys not to be in the same position of authority she and Alvan had been in the first time around. She wasn't "in the loop" in the way she had been before and she wasn't in a decision-making role, which may have bothered her.

Old habits die hard and before long, Ardys took to her bed. Perhaps the very sounds and smells of the African community served as a trigger for the depression that had engulfed her in Macha previously.

"I guess I just assumed she was down because she was out of her regular surroundings," Erma Jean, now 73, said. "I really had to pull things out of her, even to get her out of bed. I remember going and visiting her and encouraging her to play the piano. She would."

Because of her nursing background, Erma Jean said she didn't find it odd to reach out to help Ardys, even though she didn't know her well. She recalls coming into the house, seeing Ardys sitting on a chair, doing nothing. She doesn't recall talking about why Ardys was depressed; she doesn't remember Ardys talking much at all.

Although they lived next door to the Thumas at Macha, they can't remember having any personal interaction with Alvan, which seems odd, they acknowledged.

As usual, Alvan kept busy with his work and didn't acknowledge his wife's problems to anyone in the community. Once again, Ardys was left with no one to confide in, save perhaps Erma Jean who tried but failed to get this esteemed missionary wife to talk.

"He certainly didn't talk about his feelings. It was sort of like he learned to be oblivious to the depression," Esther Spurrier said. "An intense togetherness is forced on couples in the bush; for some, that becomes a gift; for others, it becomes intolerable."

"I think we project onto them what we think – that she felt sidelined or out of the limelight that year. She would have depressive episodes, but there were times when she was full of energy," John Spurrier said. "He was tolerant of her, but they didn't really have a close relationship from what I saw."

Back home in Ohio, Phil was finding out himself just how demanding a career in medicine could be of a family man. "We have often said that year was a wake-up call for our marriage, and it taught me to better balance time with family. I did enjoy the medical work involved with family practice immensely, but I was ready to move on when Mom and Dad came back," Phil said.

In Arcanum, Phil was making a name for himself as a fine doctor. "Phil became a colleague and became very deeply respected by our hospital community," Sam Brubaker said. "He's a person of stellar character, but he's a little more his mom's personality . . . he projected himself a little more than his dad. If he knew something that was pertinent to a situation, he'd be quick to share it and you knew he knew what he was talking about."

Just before Alvan and Ardys went to Macha that year, Sam Brubaker had taken his family to Macha and seen firsthand the works of Alvan's hands.

"I was impressed; this man not only knows how to practice medicine but how to lay out and design a hospital suitable for that kind of cultural economic setting. I said to myself, 'Al Thuma thought big,'" Sam said.

While at Macha, Sam and his family had become endeared to Marie Traver, a young Canadian nurse who was beloved by African nurses, students, women – everyone.

Tragedy struck while Alvan was there. In September of that year, she contracted malaria and died. Her caregivers would have included Al Thuma.

The young nurse's death occurred just several days after John Spurrier's arrival. "She went to a meeting of some sort where she got a lot of bites, presumed bed bugs. When she returned she had fever and then turned jaundiced with yellow eyes," John recalled. An initial malaria smear was negative so it was thought she might have hepatitis. However, when she got worse, the smear was repeated and it was positive

"They treated her but to no avail. By the time we arrived, she was unconscious," John said.

"I remember writing a letter to Al saying how painful it must've been," Sam said. In characteristic Thuma fashion, he did not hear anything back from Alvan expressing any emotion over it.

Ardys, however, wrote a lovely tribute that was published in the October issue of the "Evangelical Visitor," called "And God Called Her."

She was only 22, but she had given God everything, even to leaving friends and loved ones to serve God in Central Africa.

Nurses were needed badly at Macha Hospital and she came.

Eight months of service was to be her contribution! She gave it gladly. And then God took her to live with Him forever.

She was only 22.
She could have been my daughter or yours.
"To God be the glory, great things He hath done."

Ardys had only known Marie less than two months, and yet she clearly mourned her death. Who knows how much this untimely death could have contributed to Ardys' depression rearing its untimely head once again?

When summer of 1976 came, Alvan left Zambia and the good work he had begun for the last time. When his dad returned from Zambia, Phil and Elaine had decided to commit to a term of service at Macha and they left soon afterwards.

Alvan never expressed a desire to go back and family guessed it was because he couldn't handle the adulation he got there.

"Dad never wanted to be treated like a god; perhaps that's why he never went back. He was uncomfortable with the reverence and the adulation," Elaine said.

Ardys, true to form, painted over her year at Macha with a brush dipped in blessings and thankfulness as she wrote a summary of their visit for the "Evangelical Visitor.

"To return to our former home and church and see so many faithful and mature Christians – old, young and middle-aged; to share with them in church services Sunday after Sunday and at General Conference at Choma Secondary School . . . these were blessed shared experiences. To teach at Macha Secondary School, helping influence and mold young lives; to share my thoughts in morning prayers; to share together in prayer and Bible study groups as well as singing groups . . . these and many more activities were sharing experiences of invaluable worth to me personally."

Ardys went on to share that she and Alvan had participated in a Married People's Retreat in Choma along with 59 other couples. She was particularly taken with the pastor's sermon theme: "Our Homes – Are they truly Christian?" She called it "very timely." Whether she meant timely for the Zambian couples in attendance or timely for her own home, we cannot know.

But she ended her piece with a plea to pray for Christian homes – "that God may give wisdom, guidance and love in these homes, that they may stand steadfast and secure despite the storms and winds of change that are all around."

Could she have sensed that storms were brewing over her own home and that winds of change would blow in over the next two decades and change her life immeasurably once again?

In the ensuing years, Ardys would return to Macha one more time in 1984 but never again for such a long period of time and never again with her husband at her side.

Ciindi coonse tukamumanine imilimo Mwami,
Atwaambilane aluyando lwakwe,
Mbube kwaakumana ukukala kwesu kwa'nsi ano,
Nobaya kwiitwa boonse, njooba ko.

Let us labor for the Master from the dawn till setting sun,
Let us talk of all His wondrous love and care;
Then when all of life is over, and our work on earth is done,
And the roll is called up yonder, I'll be there.

Chapter Nine
When the Roll is Called Up Yonder

"Philip!"

"Mom? What's the matter?" It didn't take any special magical powers on Phil's part to deduce his mother was upset the moment he answered the phone.

"Your father . . . He doesn't seem to be himself," Ardys replied, exhaling a sigh in Ohio that immediately reached Phil's ears in Pennsylvania.

"What do you mean? What's he like?" Phil asked.

"He's a bit confused . . . weak . . . He was in the bathroom and I found him on the floor . . . Phil, should I call 911?" she said. "He's not himself at all."

Figuring that his father couldn't be in crisis or his mother wouldn't be calling another state for advice on calling 911, Phil urged her to wait and see for a bit.

"Maybe he just fainted. Wait a little bit and see how he seems," Phil suggested, thinking that perhaps his dad had suffered a vasovagal attack that may have caused him to faint. Only a doctor would know this was a possibility among the elderly.

161

When Alvan didn't improve in a few hours, Ardys called 911. It turned out Alvan had suffered a small stroke and was eventually admitted to Good Samaritan Hospital in Dayton. In order to see his dad for himself, Phil drove to Ohio the next day and was relieved to see his dad was looking pretty good. Maybe they had dodged a bullet.

Although doctors wanted to do a procedure to clean out his carotid artery – a carotid endarterectomy - Alvan refused, remembering that his brother-in-law had gotten worse after having that procedure. Doctors prescribed several days of physical therapy and sent Alvan home.

Within the week, Alvan had a much larger stroke and life for Alvan and Ardys changed forever.

Drastically weakened on one side, it became immediately clear that farming and Alvan's new physical limitations would not mix well. Once again, Phil and Elaine made the trip to Ohio, where Alvan was now a patient at Greenville Hospital.

It fell to Phil to tell his dad the difficult news.

"Dad, you know it's not really realistic for you to have the sheep and cattle now," Phil ventured. "You can't care for them."

"Yes," Alvan readily agreed. No sense fighting his logic and pure fact.

As the fall of 1997 went by, it became clear that Alvan wasn't going to gain back the strength he needed to mow the grass, tend the garden or care for his pond of fish either.

"Dad was paralyzed after the second stroke and he gradually regained some strength, but he had residual weakness for the rest of his life," Phil said. He was able to get around for some time using a cane or walker, but his physical strength was depleted.

With the animals gone and the farm work beyond their father's ability, the Thuma children started talking to their parents about selling the farm and moving to a retirement home. At first, Alvan wanted to move to the Brethren Home in Greenville, but with Phil and Wanda close to Messiah Village in Mechanicsburg Pa., it seemed to make the most sense to move there.

Alvan seemed to accept the stroke of misfortune with grace. "I remember him saying that it was an act of God that this stroke befell him. He didn't express any objection and he coped with it," said Sam Brubaker.

"I think it was very hard for Dad to leave Ohio, but he never argued. He said, 'What can you do? You bow your head and accept it,'" Wanda said.

Phil never saw his father shed a tear over losing the farm or his beloved animals. "I knew he felt bad to give them up, and at first, he probably hoped that he would recover full function, but he was realistic enough to know that selling them was the best thing to do. For sure Mom would not know how to care for them; she had never shown any interest in helping with them . . . In fact, as I sit and think about it, I can hardly ever recall seeing my dad shed a tear or cry about anything. Remember his mantra: 'Grin and bear it.'"

In the spring of 1998, the Thumas sold their farm things in an auction. Sam Brubaker was there and bought a few of Alvan's hand tools and his riding mower. The farm itself was sold to a young Old Order German Baptist couple. No one in the Thuma family wanted or could afford to buy Uncle Jake's farm and Alvan needed the money it would bring in order to afford to live at Messiah Village.

"Mom at first said she was happy and quite willing to sell the farm and move to Messiah Village, where she knew former missionaries and other old friends. Farm living would never have been her first choice. I am sure she agreed to do it for Dad. We went out to help her pack up the farm, and she seemed to be in a very good mood, while Dad was more quiet and somber," Phil recalled.

At Messiah Village, Alvan and Ardys set up housekeeping in a one-bedroom apartment but soon moved to a two-bedroom size. Alvan used his cane or walker to get around; he thought buying a motorized wheel chair showed poor stewardship of resources.

Always used to being the strong one, Alvan seemed to sense that the order of the pack was changed and he accepted it with characteristic stoicism. Ardys became the decision maker and the one to hold together their changing relationship. "He knew he wasn't what he used to be and he willingly handed it over to her," Wanda said.

"One time I was visiting Doc and I said, 'Al, what's wrong? You were so big and burly.' He said, 'Well, the body doesn't always behave itself,'" Keith Ulery recalled.

Ardys and Alvan at their Messiah Village apartment

The Thumas received many guests during their years at Messiah Village and found themselves reunited with missionaries and friends from years past who also found themselves at Messiah Village in their sunset years.

Sam and Lucy Brubaker were among their visitors. Alvan was pleased to show the flowering plants he was nurturing and Ardys gave them a tour of the buildings. "They seemed happy," Sam recalled. "In one of our later visits with Ardys, she spoke about how difficult it was for Al to deal with Meryl's separation. A husband and wife just didn't live separately. I had the feeling that she was more accepting and tolerant of that," he said.

Former Ohio doctor colleague Jesse Heise remembered the last time he stopped by Messiah Village to see Alvan, who remarked that he felt "honored" that Jesse had taken the time. "Alvan was a model Christian, very sincere and had all the qualities of a good man," he said.

Rich and Kathy Steubing would come see them when they came home on furlough.

Rich remembers giving a presentation at Messiah Village once and Alvan rose from his wheelchair to correct a statement Rich made on an incorrect date. The last time they saw Ardys, Wanda was pushing her around in a wheelchair at the Village.

"We probably saw them at their best; at the pinnacle of their careers," Rich said. "We were very privileged to have been with them at that time."

Ron Herr remembers that his uncle Alvan loved to discuss Africa while Ardys preferred to focus conversation on the family. Ron's sister, Eleanor Poe, told him that Alvan had said to her: "I was praying to God that I wouldn't dream because I dream of Zambia and then I cannot sleep."

It was in these days that Phyllis Saltzman said she began to notice a change in how her sister and brother-in-law related to each other.

"We really saw a change in Alvan – his treatment of Ardys. He was very controlling and demeaning. He'd interrupt her and correct her on almost all her facts. She would usually respond sweetly but every now and then, she'd bristle. We'd tell her to just stand up to him. She would cry about it," Phyllis said.

Marilyn Ebersole, who served as a medical technologist at in the lab at Macha from 1977 to 1989, (and later became one of the chaplains at Messiah Village) saw the Thumas often at the Village.

She would often chat with Alvan when he was out tending to his small garden plot at the Village. "Alvan was a very humble man. He didn't really talk much about his wonderful accomplishments. He loved to garden. I would ask him about the gardening he did while they were in Ohio and he would talk on and on about that, not himself," she said.

As always, Ardys was the storyteller and one who enjoyed stories too, Marilyn recalled.

"Ardys really liked me to tell her stories about my experiences with Jenny and the twins (Michael and Eric, born to Elaine and Phil while they were at Macha). Ardys lost her eyesight (due to macular degeneration) and that was something that she really minded. She talked a lot about putting up with that," she said. "You know, Ardys was the outgoing one. I could get her going about growing up. She didn't have the easiest life, so separated from family, so that she really treasured her own family. She was very close to her sisters even though they lived on the west coast. And her own children were so special to her. I think her parents leaving her here really left a scar on her that stayed with her."

After about three years, Alvan worsened and was moved to skilled nursing care while Ardys continued to live in the apartment. Their married life together in the same physical space was over; some argue their emotional closeness as a couple had ended much earlier.

"She felt like people expected her to go be with him all day long, but she wanted to do her own thing," Phil said. "From my point of view, the relationship was over."

However, in a 2005 interview about her husband's life, Ardys said, "Alvan has deteriorated. It's very hard not to be living together." Whether she said this because, as always, she was concerned about appearances or whether part of her felt this was true, we can't know.

Ardys cared deeply about what other people thought of her and felt she was being judged by onlookers over how much devotion she showed to her husband.

"She had to walk to the personal care unit from their apartment because she had given up driving due to her poor eyesight. She was always wondering if she was going to see him enough," Elaine recalled. It was easily a quarter mile walk to reach her husband's building.

"She was always concerned with other people's opinions of her. I don't know that Al was affirming enough of her," said sister Marylou Bert, who talked with Ardys weekly on the phone.

When Ardys was invited to take a trip back to India with her sisters in 2004, she declined, convinced that her place was at Messiah Village near her husband

Alvan wearing Zambian medal

Although Macha was far away in miles, it remained close in thought. In 2003, Alvan was presented the Distinguished

Service Order medal by the Zambian government in recognition of his work there. It is seldom given to a white man. Dick and Esther Miller, volunteering with Brethren in Christ World Missions in Choma at the time, received the medal in Alvan's place.

His nephew, Ron Herr carried his citation, sash and medallion back from Zambia and delivered them to Alvan, who was mostly bedbound by that point.

"We brought you something from Zambia, from the president," Ron told him.

"Oh yeah, I heard something about that," Alvan joked. "Is it made in China?"
Ron says he flipped it over; "Yup!"

Ron showed it to Alvan and asked him where he should put it and Alvan said, "Just put it in that drawer." He was not anxious to display it, Ron said.

On the windowsill in his room, however, sat a jar of red dirt that his grandsons – Wanda's sons, Malcolm and Duncan, – had collected on a visit to Macha with their parents the previous year. The boys had given one jar of Macha dirt to their grandpa and one to their grandma. Although Alvan would never again run his fingers through the soils of Zambia, he could see it from his bed.

Alvan spent seven years in nursing care at Messiah Village. At the end, he suffered from memory loss and dementia.

When her own health deteriorated, Ardys first moved to an apartment in the main building under assisted living and got around with a walker. Then, in 2007, she also moved to nursing care when she developed severe weakness in her lower limbs such that she fell frequently; later, she could no longer walk and get around independently. In nursing care, she at first was moved to a room to be near Alvan on the same wing, but not in the same room. They would continue to eat together at the same table until the last five months of Alvan's life.

When her husband really declined, Ardys became a virtual widow. Her life as she knew it was over and like many older people, she was grieving the loss of many things she treasured:

Her marriage relationship, her eyesight, her physical strength, her independence, her driver's license; really, any sense of control.

The circumstances could easily make the heartiest of souls dejected. Depression once again settled over Ardys and she would take to her bed for a week at a time, Wanda said.

"Even at Messiah Village, she wouldn't want to see a doctor when I suggested it because she said they would just put her on medication," Wanda said. "'I'm not the only one who's ever been depressed,' she would say and I would try to point out that it wasn't normal to just want to stay in bed all day for weeks."

When she did take her medicine correctly, there was improvement in her mood.

As an adult, Phil had never broached the subject of depression with his mom until she was at Messiah Village. Finally, he said, she seemed more open to talking about it and he had the courage to bring it up. "She knew she was depressed and she would take her meds more regularly," Phil said. "I remember one day she said to me that she had just had a visitor who said she just needed to pray more and get right with the Holy Spirit and it would get better." That made Phil mad, he recalls.

"That's when I became much more a defender of my mother," he said.

When Ruth Sentz and her husband moved into Messiah Village, Ardys was one of the first people to welcome her and the two became "like sisters," Ruth would later say.

"She and I just clicked. She knew she could let her hair down with me," said Ruth, who still lives at Messiah Village. "She'd call and ask me to come up. She always had some kind of refreshment for me. Invariably we talked about the past. Ardys was a goldmine, such a breadth of understanding of her time."

They spoke of the political climate in Zambia when Ardys was there, of the pioneering medical work Alvan accomplished and the legacy he had left. For Ruth, who knew little about Africa, being with Ardys expanded her worldview beyond anything she could have imagined.

There wasn't much that Ruth didn't know about Ardys, including her despair at being left behind by her parents when they returned to India, her struggle with depression, her feelings of inferiority, her doubts that she had truly lived up to the call that she felt God had put on her life.

It seemed that finally, in the sunset of her life, Ardys found the heart-to-heart girlfriend that had eluded her all those years in Africa when her housekeepers never knew her to have a friend. Years after Ardys' death, Ruth would say she felt like part of her died too.

"We had many conversations about their work in Africa. She told me she would get depressed about what she felt were misunderstandings about what they were doing," Ruth said. "One day, she felt so bereft. She felt she had missed her calling from God. But then she said, 'When the time comes to go, all will be well' and I felt like personally she was giving me assurance for my life."

Diane Barbin, a Mechanicsburg resident who volunteered at Messiah Village for 10 years, also forged an unusually close relationship with Ardys at the end of her life. It began with Diane reading missionary newsletters to Ardys, which naturally opened the door for conversations about Ardys' own missionary life.

"She just had such a heart for God. I would spend time with her and I felt a connection with her at a different level than with anyone else there," Diane said. "She was very real about her experiences as a missionary. She was grateful for all she had been able to see, but it was difficult."

Ardys opened up to Diane about her relationship with her husband. "She admired and respected him, but she in some ways found him to be a difficult man," Diane said.

In his last years, Alvan lost the strength to walk or even stand with help. By the last year or so his left side was essentially completely paralyzed and he could no longer turn himself over in bed.

"My recollection is that it was his left side that was weak from the stroke, since he still had a strong handshake with his right hand until near the end of his life. When he was at Messiah Village and moved from the apartment to the assisted living section as he got weaker, he never really talked about how he felt emotionally. His fairly constant 'mantra' as we were growing as kids was "grin and bear it" – and he lived that out himself to his dying days, never really complaining about much of anything," Phil said.

While in nursing care, Alvan was diagnosed as 'depressed' and put on antidepressants, which Phil recalls, he did not want to take. "I recall a conversation with him in which he told me that he did not think his situation should be called 'depression' but rather he was just 'discouraged' given his circumstances, because he could no longer do the things he was used to doing," Phil said. His father was well acquainted with the process of aging, having seen it firsthand in his days as medical director of the Brethren Retirement Home back in Greenville.

In the seven years he was in nursing care, Wanda said she thinks her dad probably wondered sometimes why he was still here. "I believe however that there was meaning and purpose to his life in those last several years; I know he was a sounding board for me," she would say later at his funeral. "I would watch Lawrence Welk with him on a Saturday evening, and then tell him what I'd been doing in my graduate classes. I would babble about papers I was required to write on esoteric concepts in academia, or mull over my thesis proposal. Invariably, when I left I had a clearer idea of what I needed to do and was so grateful for his advice – although he usually hadn't said a word!"

Still true to his characteristic frugality, Alvan initially declined offers for cataract surgery and for hearing aids because, he said, he was going to die and what did he need them for in the meantime anyway?

While Alvan seemed able to accept – and even expect – his deteriorating physical condition, Ardys lamented the effects of aging.

"She would say she never thought growing old would be like this . . . and I would say, 'What did you expect?' Your body ages; this is what happens,'" said Wanda, referring to her mother's macular degeneration, which took her eyesight little by little and spinal stenosis that landed her in a wheelchair for four years in skilled nursing at the end of her life.

Thuma family after holiday meal at Messiah Village

To volunteer Diane Barbin, however, Ardys was a pillar of gratitude, even as her eyes and her legs betrayed her. "Her vision was going and her circumstances weren't the best, but she'd say, 'That's OK. I had such a great life and God blessed me so much.' I thought to myself, 'She's relegated to this and she can still be grateful?' So many people there are bitter. She was not."

For many years, the Thuma children had all family holiday meals in one of the Messiah Village meeting rooms so that both Alvan and Ardys could be together with the family. Ardys would come out to Phil or Wanda's house a few times during the year, but not often. The last family get-together she regularly attended was the annual family fruit cake-making at either Wanda's or Phil's house over the Thanksgiving weekend. The last time the couple was out together was to the wedding of Jenny Thuma, Phil and Elaine's daughter, at Dillsburg BIC Church in 2001.

Barb saw her parents two to three times a year but talked on the phone to her mom every week. Barb still misses those phone calls. In the fall of 2007, Ardys went to Indiana to see Barb, who is an educator with Purdue Extension in Fort. Wayne, Indiana. Wanda thinks she realized this would be the last time she would travel.

In the spring of 2009, before they returned to Macha, Phil and Elaine said their goodbyes to Alvan. They never knew when they left if it might be their final good-bye, but this time it seemed more a possibility.

As Wanda watched her father's condition deteriorate, she finally addressed it with her dad, suggesting, "Dad, it seems like you've got 'the dwindles.'"

He eyed her intently and, without emotion, replied, "I am very old, you know."

Wanda wanted to engage hospice but needed a doctor's order. Finally, after weight loss was noted, the doctor pronounced "failure to thrive" and hospice was ordered. Dementia had set in by this point. Alvan still knew Wanda and Ardys, but his memory of Macha or that he was a doctor was gone.

"When I visited him, I'd always greet him and tell him who I was – just a little reminder – and he knew me. I'd do most of the talking, telling him about my thesis or news from Phil and Elaine," Wanda said.

In early August 2009, Alvan slipped into a coma. Wanda and Ardys kept a vigil by his bed. On the evening of August 12, Ardys took a break from his bedside to get ready for bed. Seeing her father's breaths become shallow, Wanda began to say aloud an old Celtic prayer,

Christ stands before you.
and peace is in his mind.

Sleep, O sleep in the calm of all calm.
Sleep, O sleep in the loves of all loves.
Sleep this night in the God of all life.
Amen.

Wanda held her father's hand as he slipped peacefully away.

Silenced were his many stories of exploits meant more to entertain than bring self-glory. Absent was the heart that saw people as people, not as black or white, educated or uneducated, rich or poor. Gone was the man whose life demonstrated again and again his vital belief that actions, not words, served as one's best testimony to the Lord. Yet here on earth, oceans away from where his still body lay, a bustling hospital was saving lives, improving health and bearing witness always to the impact this humble farming doctor had left on a patch of ground in rural Africa.

In Macha that August day, Phil was busy preparing for a large training conference in connection with the Malaria Research Institute at Macha, which opened in 2005. He knew from a phone call from his sister that death was imminent.

"Phil wasn't crazy about being at the conference, with all those important people," Elaine said. "Now we joke that this was Dad's last gift . . . that Phil wouldn't have to be at that conference."

As they drove out past the hospital for their flight home, Phil and Elaine stopped to shake the hands of what seemed like the entire hospital staff lined up out front in a unified show of respect. Even now, Elaine gets tears in her eyes at the memory.

Alvan's memorial service in Pennsylvania took place on Aug. 19 at the Messiah Village BIC Church. In her opening remarks, Wanda said what everyone who knew Alvan probably could agree with: "I suspect if my father had his druthers about where and how he died, it would have been on his farm, perhaps while digging dahlias or spider lilies in his garden, or while smoking his bee hives spread all over the county, or even while throwing hay down for his Dorset sheep herd."

Alvan's life of service to others was highlighted again and again by those who honored him after his death.

Grandchildren carrying Alvan's coffin at his burial

Said Phil, "In Zambia, as I have talked to people over the years who knew him during his years of service there, they repeatedly talk about how he worked with people and did not just supervise them. Whether that meant he helped lay the bricks for a new hospital, or helped to pull the deep well pump when it went bad, he rarely expected people to do things that he was not also willing to do himself. This servant attitude came through even when he was the medical superintendent of the large university teaching hospital in the capital city, Lusaka. He was often known to leave his office and help in the busy outpatient clinic, working side by side with the junior doctors."

In a symbolic gesture that brought Macha a little closer to Alvan's final resting place, the Thuma siblings decided to offer mourners the chance to sprinkle a little of the red dirt from Alvan's windowsill jar onto his grave.

Dorothy Gish remembers the feeling of that moment years later. "I found it very meaningful. It was a way of recognizing a significant part of his life," she said.

They also sang Tonga hymns organized by Elaine at the graveside. Later that evening, some of the family went back to the cemetery and helped to shovel in as much dirt as they could. In Africa, it is customary to do so. "It was raining," Wanda recalled, "And it seemed fitting that the heavens were crying with us."

The Macha community would show their respect for Alvan formally on Aug. 24 of that year, when they held a memorial service that drew some 200 people to the Primary Health Care building on the Macha campus. Among those in attendance were Chief Macha, past and present bishops and leaders of the BIC Church, more than 20 of the local headmen from villages surrounding Macha, more than 50 nursing students as well as many hospital staff and community members.

"The outpouring from the community was amazing," Elaine said, remembering not only the service but the many expressions of sympathy the family received.

They poured themselves out for the family of a man who had first poured himself out for them and modeled firsthand what Jesus meant in Matthew 26: "For whatever you do for the least of these, you do for me."

Chief Macha recognized the fact that not only Macha benefitted from Dr. Thuma, but all of Zambia and even Africa had as well.

With humor, he noted the physical labor that Alvan poured into the hospital. "He actually brought bricks up to build the hospital. I wouldn't like to say he was naughty, but he guesses he was because bringing bricks was punishment every Saturday," he said with a laugh.

The memorial service attested to "how much love we have for Dr. Thuma," Chief Macha said, and with good humor, he asked Phil to demonstrate the same love his father showed and have the next doctor in place at Macha before he retires.

Mukuwa Kalambo, then executive director of Macha Mission Hospital and currently managing director of Macha Research Trust, called Alvan "a doctor of great distinction" and "a person of rare qualities." He noted that the impact Alvan left on the community could be seen in the number of people there who are named after him, including the Bishop of the Zambian BIC Church.

Representing the Thuma family, Ron Herr reflected on what Alvan's parents might have thought about their son's life and legacy. "Their philosophy of life was that they valued education and were service-oriented people," a trait they passed on to many of their children who became teachers, nurses, doctors. "I think they would've said 'That's my son. Mission accomplished; a life of service to God,'" he said.

At his memorial service, the new Alvan E. Thuma House of Hope was unveiled as the new name of the AIDS clinic "so that the members of our staff and the patients that will come will forever remember him," Kalambo said.

The AIDS clinic is the only building on the medical campus that bears a name. "Phil only let them do it because his dad was dead," John Spurrier said. "He knew his dad wouldn't want that kind of recognition."

Many of the Thuma family were present for the Macha memorial service that day, including Alvan's granddaughter Lynette Thuma who was spending two months there as a doctor.

"I was very appreciative to Macha and her people for the way they honored Grandpa at his memorial service; it was very meaningful," she said. "I have been to Macha on three separate occasions, once as a medical student for four weeks, then as a resident for six weeks and then my last visit as a physician. Each time has been just as difficult dealing with the sick and dying, knowing sometimes there isn't much I can do. On the other hand, I have felt welcomed by everyone who either knew Grandpa or Grandma or heard of them or my dad ... My dream was to follow in Grandpa and Grandma's legacy of missionary medicine, but it just didn't happen. With each trip to Macha, I just felt I couldn't go through with it."

Although it's impossible to say with certainty what the death of Alvan meant to Ardys, it's clear that the man she knew – and the life they shared – had been gone far in advance of his physical death.

"Their relationship had already changed once he moved over to nursing and she stayed in the apartment so that when he died, it wasn't a huge change," Barb said. "He already wasn't around, wasn't talkative . . . She had already grieved that loss."

Her sister, Marylou, said they talked once a week on the phone without fail. It became a struggle for Ardys to call her because she couldn't see the digits on the phone as her macular degeneration worsened, Marylou said.

Phyllis and Ardys talked on the phone every couple of weeks. Her younger sister got the impression she was involved with a lot of things at the Village.

Remembers Elaine, "Mom lost the ability to walk, which was hard on her. She could still tell great stories and loved it when people came to visit."

Her mind wandered easily back to Africa.

Joe Ginder, who had lost touch with the Thumas, looked up Ardys when he was at the Village visiting his own parents just a couple of months before Ardys died. "She wanted to talk about the days at Macha," he said.

Wanda was convinced her mother could go on for years in nursing care; she was in good health, generally speaking.

One Friday evening in June 2011, Ardys began complaining of chest pain and was transported from the Village to nearby Holy Spirit Hospital, where it was learned that she had suffered a massive heart attack. With Phil and Wanda by her side, she listened to the doctor explain all the technologies available to help her heart and she dismissed all of them. "I don't need that," she said and signed a "Do Not Resuscitate" order. She told her children to go home and get some sleep; she would see them tomorrow.

Later that evening, Ardys was chatty with the nurses, even bragging about Wanda's recently-earned doctoral degree. "Maybe that's an example of her life in a nutshell," Wanda said later, "Gregarious almost to the point of embarrassment sometimes for my more introverted personality, my mother loved to talk and make connections with people, no matter which part of the world she was in."

Barb recalls calling her mom in the hospital that evening and how they laughed together when Ardys noted that one of her doctors was of Indian descent.

"She told me she was feeling better and we agreed on a time when I would call her the next day," Barb said. She knew when she heard Phil's voice on the other end of the phone in the middle of the night that she would never speak to her mom again.

Family helping fill grave at funeral for Ardys

In the wee hours of June 19, Ardys had a fatal arrhythmia and the nurses honored her DNR order signed the day before.

The hurt little girl who had turned her own grief into compassion for others, who had striven above all else to follow God's call on her life, who had repeatedly put others' needs before her own as fledgling missionary, gracious hostess, exuberant teacher, was finally at peace. The depression that seemed always to lap at her heels finally laid down forever.

At her memorial service at Messiah Village, her children lauded their mother for her courage to overcome fear and rejection, her drive to educate herself and others and also, for the first time publicly, they talked about her ugly foe – depression.

For many in the room, giving voice to what they had seen in Ardys was no surprise. For others, some of them family, there was the fervent wish that her children had remained silent. But to remain silent, they felt, was to give her depression the final victory. No, Christ had the final victory in Ardys Thuma's life and to Him be the glory for every day she had pulled herself up and out of its dark clutches.

"While my mother had her own 'thorn in the flesh' manifested throughout her life as recurrent bouts of depression, she was able, despite that 'thorn,' to be a wonderful mother, wife and friend to many," Phil said. "I know that the Lord used her in numerous ways to touch many people's lives, and the fact that all of her children are followers of Christ is probably the greatest tribute to her life of nurturing, teaching, concern and prayers for us as a mother."

At her graveside, as at Alvan's, those who wished were given the chance to sprinkle red dirt onto the lowered casket, burying with Ardys part of her beloved yet exacting Macha.

----- 🦣 -----

Kwiina buusu, Jesu nguwangu,
Kulabila bubotu bwa-Leza;
Makani akwe, muulo wakwe,
Musalwi 'Muuya, ndasanzigwa.

Blessed assurance, Jesus is mine!
O what a foretaste of glory divine!
Heir of salvation, purchase of God,
born of his Spirit, washed in his blood.

Makani angu, Jesu nguwangu!
Ndalumba Mwami ciindi coonse.

This is my story, this is my song,
Praising my Savior all the day long

Chapter Ten
Blessed Assurance: This is My Story

The first year. It's nearly behind us. And that's a really good feeling. It's a good feeling because we're still here. I can't say that I always knew we were going to make it this far. Some days I was ready to throw in the towel in the form of buying a one-way ticket back 'home.'

I've learned that moving is a long-term transitioning process. For me, it's been full of emotions that presented themselves in all sorts of ways. At all sorts of times. And I often felt like I was incapable of controlling them. That was scary for me. I've cried more tears. Threw more pity-parties for myself. And used more choice words than ever before. I've spent more days inside our home than outside. Too worried, self-conscious, and unprepared to leave.

When you're being 'sent out' by a lot of very supportive people under the label 'missionary,' it comes with its fair share of pressure. And that pressure sometimes felt like a heavier load than I was able to carry. And I didn't want to be fake. And I didn't want to disappoint. And I didn't want to fail.

And it's embarrassing to say, my response to these challenges has not led me to Jesus. Sometimes I felt so far from Jesus I didn't know how to get back. I felt like I was drowning.

I didn't really want Jesus but I wanted to start enjoying life here. I was attempting to ask for the wisdom to live in Macha yet I was all sorts of unstable and my loyalty was far from the Jesus I was asking the wisdom from.

I wanted to immediately like it here. I wanted it to feel like home. I wanted to stop missing things back in the States. I wanted to know, beyond a shadow of a doubt, that Macha was supposed to be home. And when those feelings didn't transpire at the timeline I had hoped, I started asking a lot of 'why' questions: Why here. Why this. Why that. Why me. And more often than any other question, I asked 'Why in the world am I not better at living here?' I wasn't learning Tonga quick enough. I wasn't making enough friends. I wasn't feeling like myself.

All that to say, it has been a really hard year.

BUT! (And I am SO glad there is a 'BUT') I can say with confidence that things have shifted and gotten worlds better.

I started having meaningful conversations. I've found one of the best friends a person could ask for. Communication between Eric and I has gotten exceedingly better (when I had already thought it was plenty good.) Jesus and I reconnected. And watching our girls grow in this place has been the most amazing gift.

It's a privilege to write this post because it's been the privilege of this lifetime to live here. It's been the most difficult year. It's been the most challenging year. And it's been the most influential year. I think that correlation is worth recognizing.

Here's to year two.

- *Corie Thuma, blog post, August 15, 2014*

More than 40 years after Alvan and Ardys Thuma left Zambia, their footprints linger as yet another family member's life takes root in the African soil. This time, it is grandson Eric Thuma, son of Phil and Elaine. He and his wife, Corie, and their two small children, Charlotte and Reece, moved to Macha in August 2013 to begin serving with Push the Rock, a ministry aimed at sharing the love and message of Christ through sports.

"I don't spend much time thinking about legacy, though I am certainly proud of my grandfather and father and feel blessed to have the Thuma name in a community where that means by default, people trust us as PTR Zambia," Eric said. "I can say that it is kind of fun to be a Thuma and not a doctor here, where so many people hear Thuma and assume doctor."

The word "legacy" can't help but come up when thinking about the Thumas' impact on the Macha community. What would it look like had Alvan Thuma never gone there?

"His life here at Macha helped make Macha different," said Mukuwa Kalambo, managing director of Macha Research Trust. "Thuma was really a household name and there was no one to compare him to; at that time, he was THE doctor. There was none like him. He was like a savior."

And, Kalambo said, more than a half century later, "Dr. Thuma is still doing good for this community --- people are really talking about what Phil has done with malaria control and now, with Eric, coming, the legacy of Dr. Thuma continues."

Thanks to Alvan Thuma, today some 160,000 people in the African bush have access to medical care at the hospital he started. Although the main part of the one-story building remains much as it was when he was there – the men's ward to the left and the women's ward to the right – there have been many additions. At the back of the hospital, there are outpatient, maternity, pediatric and tuberculosis wards.

Although Phil Thuma once said he would never become a doctor, his decision to follow in his dad's footsteps elongated the footprints of his family into Macha for who knows how many generations to come.

In 1976, he and Elaine answered the BIC Mission Board's request to give Macha Hospital two years of voluntary service. They decided they liked it well enough to consider returning, but to do what?

"God put the children of Africa on my heart," Phil recalls. "I feel responsible to see that kids in Africa, particularly

Macha, have a chance to grow up, regardless of measles, malaria or HIV." After a three-year pediatrics residency at Johns Hopkins University and a year as chief resident in pediatrics there, he returned with his wife, Elaine, to Macha to be a full-time missionary.

"It was a tough decision," he admitted. "Do you work in a place where you'll be a 'Dr. Phil' rather than 'Dr. Thuma' because there's only one Dr. Thuma? I knew from the year working in Ohio when people would call the house and say "Is the boy doctor there?" that I would live in the shadow of someone seen as a much larger person than me. Yet here, I'm accepted. In Africa, you are who you are because of who your parents are . . . do you come from good stock? My name here was a foot in the door."

He paused, then smiled, "Plus, Macha is "my home village. I'm third culture."

Elaine, herself a registered nurse, sees her most important work as supporting and encouraging her husband's work. "I never imagined myself, a girl from the small town of Dillsburg, visiting anywhere in Africa let alone living there," she said. "We often quote Psalm 115:1 as our theme song; 'Not to us, Lord, not to us but to your name be the glory, because of your love and faithfulness.'"

Today, Macha Research Trust, which operates as the Malaria Institute at Macha, employs 65 full-time staff, 62 of whom are Zambians. To be able to offer steady employment to local residents, many of whom might otherwise eke out a living with subsistence farming, is one of Phil's greatest satisfactions.

Though humble like his dad, Phil smiles when he says there were many people who thought it would be impossible to run a state-of-the-art molecular lab like this out in the bush, 40 miles from the nearest town. "But I'm stubborn enough that I love to prove people wrong," Phil said.

While his dad said only "OK" when Phil told him he was going to return to Macha as a medical missionary, Ardys didn't try to hide her pride in her son, referring to Phil's work as "an ongoing monument to Al's endeavors" in "My Story, My Song."

George Kibler, former Macha mission superintendent, echoes the sentiments of many people who are thankful for Phil's continued presence at Macha. "I think it's great. Phil has picked up the legacy of his father and is using his expertise and contacts with the medical community here in the U.S. to expand the work there. In a way, he's a chip off the old block. He loves Africa," George said.

Macha has gained an international reputation and initiated treatment approaches that are being reproduced elsewhere in the continent. There have been worldwide firsts there as well: In 2007, the Malaria Institute was the first to discover that malaria could be detected from saliva rather than just a blood sample.

Through the use of an innovative "test and treat" approach that identifies people who test positive for two of Africa's deadliest health maladies – malaria and HIV – and treats them before they have symptoms, transmission has been greatly curbed.

The proof of that is in the numbers: In 1989 when Phil, then medical officer in charge of the 208-bed hospital, first began his malaria research that would eventually attract the attention and funding of Johns Hopkins Public School of Health, malaria was the No. 1 cause of death at Macha.

By testing everyone in a village for the mosquito-borne parasite that causes malaria, Phil and his team were able to identify malaria carriers, leading to the stunning discovery that asymptomatic infected people could be treated with anti-malarial medicine and stop further transmission. Now, malaria cases there have dropped by 98 percent, with only one or two deaths a year, said Phil, who once watched two or three children a day die from malaria.

In 2001, when John Spurrier returned to service at Macha after a hiatus home in the States, AIDS was an epidemic and a death sentence. Back then, there was a funeral every week; now there may be one a month – thanks to the "test and treat" approach that identifies HIV-infected people before they get symptoms so that antiretroviral medications can be started sooner. Although the drugs are not a cure, if taken correctly, within three to five months, the virus can't be found in the blood.

Mother-to-child transmission of HIV has decreased dramatically, with HIV in newborns down from almost 15 percent in 2002 to 7.2 percent in 2012, John said. Antiretrovirals also curb transmission of HIV from an infected partner to an uninfected partner.

The impact that their efforts have had on two of their deadliest health foes isn't lost on the Zambians who live in villages surrounding the hospital.

Aaron Chidakwa, Headman of Chidakwa Village, speaks for many when he says the community has been made the better for them coming.

"At first the Macha Hospital was small, but these days, we are extending our work; keeping our eyes forward for the next thing to study. Dr. Spurrier promises we are now looking forward to the day where there will be no AIDS," he said. "And Dr. Phil Thuma had a vision . . . People are lucky in Macha because malaria is coming down."

None of their efforts, however, could have succeeded if the people of Macha had refused to work with them, to take their advice, to become an active player in their own best health.

Only one thing made that possible: Trust.

In the "test and treat' approach, it was trust in their doctors – and their longstanding presence in the community – that drew villagers to comply and get tested.

That trust began with Alvan Thuma, who built it with each brick he personally laid for Macha Hospital, each patient he personally touched when no one else ever had, each time he personally invested in a villager's life with tangible things like money and food and intangible things like compassion that looked past the color of their skin and saw in them a soul not unlike his own.

"I know there is a difference in our race, but the way Dr. Thuma used to treat us, it showed we are really just one people," said Lazarus Moono Moonga, a subsistence farmer in Macha who laid bricks for the hospital alongside Alvan.

Ardys saw her new neighbors through the same lens as her husband.

"She hosted African visitors in her home, had them drink tea from her tea cups and use her bathroom. She treated Africans as equals when their perception was that others treated them as primitive heathens," Phil said.

The emphasis on personal relationships that both Alvan and Ardys displayed just naturally caused the people of Macha to fall in love with them.

When Marilyn Ebersole served as a medical technologist at in the lab at Macha from 1977 to 1989, the Thumas were gone, but their names were still very present. "The Africans really, really revered them," she said.

Every January, Wanda, a registered nurse and associate professor of nursing at Messiah College, takes a team of Messiah nursing students to Macha. Her students walk the halls where her dad walked – and even her mom seems not so far away when she is there.

"It feels like going home in a way. Mom knew that wherever you are is home. She had the skill to make it comfy and make it yours," Wanda said.

Alvan and Ardys' children: Barb, Wanda, Phil, Meryl

Eric and Corie Thuma going to live at Macha continues the Thuma legacy another generation, a fact that's not lost on Zambians or Thumas.

"We were told that one of the biggest honors to a Zambian is when someone comes back – so for this family to continue on is a big thing to them," Elaine said. "They love us and they know we love them. There have always been Zambians alongside us; we didn't do this alone."

Says Eric, "It's a blessing to follow in the footsteps of those who paved the way. I just see us as taking advantage of the opportunity that is afforded us, and who knows, maybe our children will be able to do the same someday."

The Thumas left a legacy of embracing the changing times, taking a stand for what is morally right no matter the cost and caring little about pretense or prestige.

"They were a family who were open to innovations and new ideas. Thinking outside the box is a family trait," said Kathy Steubing, who credited Ardys as her mentor in Lusaka.

"They leave two legacies," said her husband, Rich Steubing. "One is medical; Macha is a pretty significant hospital. Two is political; they took the context very seriously, the wave of African independence in the 1960s. Other missionaries had no concept of the majority of people needing to have their own rights."

The irony is that Alvan was only in Macha for 10 years yet he is remembered and talked about as if he were there for many years, Phil said, perhaps because the fruit of his labors there has stretched across decades. "His legacy is that he was the first missionary doctor, but he was different from other missionaries here. He got down and helped shovel dirt and helped lay bricks; I don't think Zambians ever saw white missionaries do manual labor before. All they knew were the colonial white missionaries carrying a stick as a sign of authority and standing in the shade and giving orders," he said.

Although faith in God was of utmost importance to Alvan, he wasn't one to preach it; he preferred to live it and hope that others saw in him evidence of a God whom they would also want to direct their lives.

"He had a heart for other people. I never felt he ignored me to serve the Lord, but we absolutely knew my dad was committed to doing what he did because he believed God called him to do it," Phil said.

"He was a quiet example of Christian service," Rich Steubing said. "My guess is that Al saw himself as a doctor who was also a Christian and he would witness when he could but his job was not to be an evangelist."

Although he didn't always embrace his time in the pulpit, Alvan was very proud of his ordination with the BIC.

"One evening he said to me, "You know my mother had wanted me to be a minister and I thought about it. I wonder why I never did?" And I said, "Maybe your skills were elsewhere, look at all you did,"" Wanda said.

Barb was most struck by the kind-hearted, patient man her father was and the way his life mirrored his faith.

For Meryl, his father's legacy is that he taught by example. "He valued education and all four of us children went on for higher education. All four of us also serve others in our life vocation," he said, noting that he also picked up his father's talent for designing and constructing buildings, which he has done in Honduras.

Alvan was very humble about his own legacy at Macha.

"They tried to change the name of the hospital in the late 1990s, shortly after they had named Frances Davidson High School. Chief Macha said, 'Let's name the hospital after Alvan,' but I said I knew my father wouldn't like that. We had often talked about how people gave money and got buildings named after them and we thought that wasn't appropriate," Phil said. "After he died, the chief again brought this up and John (Spurrier) asked if we could name the ART clinic after him and I agreed. It's located behind the hospital and no one calls it by that name anyway."

Many parents call their children by the name "Thuma" however – so while bricks and mortar might not bear his name, there are plenty of living, breathing monuments who attest to the impact that Alvan Thuma had on the Macha community. And some of them are quite possessive about their namesake. Some years ago, Phil met a villager who was named Thuma.

"How did you get my name?" he asked Phil.

"It was my name before it was your name!" Phil replied, to the man's great surprise.

Ardys' legacy was, most agree, her hospitality, shown to Zambians, school children, house guests and fellow residents at Messiah Village.

"We can recall many instances of when she took both complete strangers and many others – of all races and creeds – into her home, and treated them with compassion and respect, no matter what they believed or did. She, together with my father, modeled to us children what it meant to follow the Biblical directive of showing love and kindness to all people, no matter what their status," Phil said.

"Her legacy is certainly one of love and compassion, very non-judgmental," agreed her sister Phyllis Saltzman. "She was a role model of dignity and positively contributed to any group was involved with."

Her sense of style – and love of matching shoes and purses – are also something many remember her by; perhaps she loved them so much because she never had them growing up.

"Grandma loved beauty. This came out in her style and jewelry," said Jenny Thuma Wetzel, Phil and Elaine's daughter, who is also a doctor. "I got several of her scarves, bracelets and necklaces after she passed. I enjoy wearing them and being reminded of her! I get so many compliments and I enjoy telling people that they were hers."

Jenny also saw her grandmother's love of beauty evidenced in the many plants she cultivated. "Grandma had an old sink in the farm kitchen where the African violets always were when we visited in the winter. The plants were huge and beautiful! She also took care of the large, ancient Christmas cactus. Grandpa told us that when he first saw it, the people who 'knew' said it was at least 70 years old, and at the time of him telling us this, it was 70 years after that!"

"Ardys was a giant of a person who really trusted Jesus. Her compassion for people was outstanding," her Messiah Village friend Ruth Sentz said.

For Messiah Village volunteer Diane Barbin, the brief imprint of Ardys Thuma on her life is unforgettable. "When Ardys was going downhill, I felt like God offered me this privilege of feeding this woman who had done so much for so many others. I'll never forget it," she said, tearing up years later. "When I walk past the hallway where her room was, I still glance down there . . . I know she had struggles . . . but she always tried."

It was important to the Thuma siblings to include their mother's depression in her biography to remove stigma that still surrounds any diagnosis associated with mental health – and to be correct. "My mother had major depression to the point of being disabled. To leave it out is dishonest," Phil said.

The many layers of their personalities have made the story of Alvan and Ardys fascinating to research and challenging to tell.

Their lives stand as testimony to the fact that God will provide the strength and grace needed for what He calls each of us to do. That doesn't mean it won't be hard or draining; that it won't bring tears and groaning, but it is a bittersweet mix of calling and surrendering and knowing you poured yourself out for God. As Alvan and Ardys themselves no doubt knew, it feels hard yet so very good.

Ardys words in "My Story, My Song" bear repeating: "A great deal of Al's and my life have gone into Macha Mission Hospital, and parts of our hearts shall always remain there with those people and that work. It was not all easy, however. There were many times of discouragement, but God always gave grace and strength. Even as I write this now, tears come to my eyes as I think of those hard, but also very precious years. Neither of us would ever give them up if we could! They stand as the upmost in our dedication to God."

Barb says she's not sure her parents ever expressly stated their core values as a family, but she certainly picked up on them: "Treat others with respect; be a person of integrity;

work hard, be a Christian and be involved in your church; your faith should permeate your life," she said.

In other words, Wanda said, "commitment." "If you feel led to do something and maybe you don't quite fit the mold – like my father and his 'irregularities' and mother not fitting the missionary mold – you still follow that lead because you don't know where it will take you."

Although Meryl is quick to recall how stoic his dad always was and how his mother's depression negatively impacted family life, he recognizes the great things they both were able to accomplish in spite of these obstacles. He appreciates the fact that his parents accepted his own imperfections and disappointments in life – his separation from his wife chief among them – without judgment or condemnation. "Nobody is perfect. We all carry a lot of baggage with us," he said. "They tried their very best and they have gone on to their reward."

The Thuma family, Phil said, will remember Alvan as "a man who lived his life transparently – and like most of us he was not a perfect human being – but he was a man of integrity, having a servant attitude, and a willingness to serve his God through word and deed."

Service above self.

Perhaps that's it. It rings true in this letter dated June 1964, from Ardys to Alvan's sister, Elizabeth Thuma, "We didn't even write to Mama before Mother's Day. Alvan usually does, but he has just been so very busy – the best gift he could give you, Mama, is what he is doing now – giving all his life for the service of God and others – and in that you can be very proud of him!"

In a little black sermon book that his children still keep, Alvan wrote out his own goals in small, precise penmanship: "I do not intend with my talents and God-given skills to stand before great crowds. I want to use my hands and my knowledge of medicine to humbly help those people by giving them a little more hope in this life and to tell them of the Hope after the grave . . . I only ask to be a sower, but if we sow, we shall also reap."

The crowds who lined up outside the hospital as a sign of respect as Phil and Elaine left Macha after Alvan's death, who paid tribute to Dr. Thuma at his memorial service and who even today are treated with life-saving surgeries at Macha Hospital and given drugs at the Alvan E. Thuma House of Hope – these are just a small representation of the harvest that came from one couple's humble obedience to God.

----- 🜚 -----

ACKNOWLEDGEMENTS

Thank you to those who shared their time and memories during the research for this book (* = deceased since interview):

Berger, Daniel
Bert, Marylou (Engle)
Bert, Sam and Erma Jean
Brubaker, Sam
Chidakwa, Aaron
Chimbongwe, Lameck
Chimbongwe, Misheck
Climenhaga, David
Ebersole, Marilyn
*Engle, Harold
Figueroa, Janae (Thuma)
*Ginder, Joe
Gish, Dorothy
Hamukang'andu, Thuma
Heise, Jesse
Herr, Ron
Kababa, Rosa
Kalambo, Mukuwa
Kazemba, Andrew
Kibler, George
Madubansi, Trywell
Miller, Edith
Moonga, Lazaurus Moono
Moono, Selina
Muchimba, Daniel
Muchimba, Jacob
*Muleya, Martha
Muleya, Stephen

Munkombwe, Ruth
*Mwaanga, Esther
*Mwaanga, Jesse
Mwaanga, Sarah
Saltzman, Phyllis (Engle)
Schwartz, Glenn
Schwartz, Verna
Sink, Cindy
Spurrier, Esther
Spurrier, John
Steckley, Norma
Stern, Mim
Steubing, Kathy
Steubing, Rich
Strayer, Millyellen
Thuma, Barb
Thuma, Elaine
Thuma, Lynette
Thuma, Phil
Thuma, Corie
Thuma, Eric
Thuma, Meryl
Thuma-McDermond, Wanda
Ulery, Keith
Worman, Bob
Worman, Winnie
Wetzel, Jenny (Thuma)

Thanks to those who served as Tonga interpreters during my visit to Zambia:

Mishek Chimbongwe
Mabel Munsaka
Mutinta Nyirenda

Esther Spurrier
Elaine Thuma

Special thanks to Olivia Kimmel for taking the present-day pictures while in Zambia.

This book was self-published by the children of Alvan and Ardys Thuma. For any editorial or factual corrections, please feel free to contact: editor@thuma.name

ABOUT THE AUTHOR

Carolyn Kimmel is a journalist who writes for newspapers and magazines, both in Pennsylvania and nationally. She has also written two books on early missionaries with the Brethren in Christ Church.

Her writing has won numerous state and national awards. Most recently, she was the first-place winner of the 2013 Amy Writing Award, given by the Amy Foundation in Lansing, Mich. in recognition of faith-based writing published in a secular news outlet. She won the award for a story she wrote about Dr. Phil Thuma and Dr. John Spurrier and their work at Macha Hospital in Zambia, which she saw firsthand when she traveled to Africa to research this book.

Carolyn lives in Dillsburg, Pa. with her husband, Mark, and three daughters.

25695401R00135

Made in the USA
Middletown, DE
07 November 2015